LITTLE WOMEN

Louisa May Alcott

AUTHORED by Elizabeth K. Panarelli
UPDATED AND REVISED by Bella Wang

COVER DESIGN by Table XI Partners LLC
COVER PHOTO by Olivia Verma and © 2005 GradeSaver, LLC

BOOK DESIGN by Table XI Partners LLC

Published by GradeSaver LLC, www.gradesaver.com

First published in the United States of America by GradeSaver LLC. 2010

ISBN 978-1-60259-239-1

Printed in the United States of America

For other products and additional information please visit
http://www.gradesaver.com

Table of Contents

Table of Contents

Biography of Alcott, Louisa May (1832-1888)

Louisa May Alcott was born on November 29, 1832, to Abigail "Abba" May Alcott and Amos Bronson Alcott. She was born in Pennsylvania, but she largely grew up near Boston and Concord, Massachusetts. Louisa had three sisters: Anna, who was older, Lizzie, who was younger, and May, the youngest.

Louisa's father was a strident philosopher in the Transcendentalist movement who tried to live by his beliefs. For one six-month period, he moved his family to a collective, experimental farm named Fruitlands where they wore only linen, since cotton was associated with slavery. The experiment, like many of Mr. Alcott's pursuits, ended with the family impoverished and moving to a new residence. Mr. Alcott opened several schools, but his controversial teaching methods, such as the Socratic Method and avoidance of corporal punishment unless the class unanimously agreed it was necessary, led parents to withdraw their students. His educational methods went on to inform modern pedagogical philosophy. Louisa often felt frustrated by her father's idealism and the strains it put on her mother and family. Louisa worked in many jobs to help keep her family afloat.

Louisa loved to write and hoped that it would one day help her support her family. She published stories in the *Saturday Evening Gazette* as a teenager. When she was 22, *Flower Fables* was published, a book of stories she wrote at 16. Her writing is often autobiographical, as in the gentle satire of her family's "Transcendental Wild Oats" or her book *Work* describing her own hardships working, published in 1873. Eager to support the war effort, Louisa served as an army nurse in 1862 and published descriptions of her experience in *Hospital Sketches* in 1863. This book had small success, enough to bring her to the attention of Thomas Niles, Jr., the editor who asked her to write the girls' novel. In response, Louisa wrote *Little Women*, her most famous work, drawing explicitly from her family's life. The character Jo's experience publishing her first novel reflected Louisa's struggle with *Moods*, published in 1865. Under pseudonyms, Louisa also published "sensation stories" in newspapers, which she wrote largely for money. Louisa was thrilled when the success of *Little Women* allowed her to pay off her family's debt.

Louisa was often frustrated with her father's idealism, but through him, she befriended the families of great thinkers and writers of the time, including Henry David Thoreau, Ralph Waldo Emerson, and Nathaniel Hawthorne. Influenced by their ideas and those of her parents, she supported equality of all people and fought for abolition of slavery and women's suffrage, in addition to being part of the temperance movement advocating abstinence from alcohol. Like the character Jo, Louisa was very independent. She never married, but did care for her niece Lulu after Lulu's mother May died. Unlike Jo, Louisa was able to travel to Europe twice, once in 1865-1866 and again in 1870-1871. She returned the day of publication of *Little Men*.

Louisa May Alcott was a prolific author, publishing over 30 books and collections of short stories. She died two days after her father, on March 6, 1888.

About Little Women

Little Women: Meg, Jo, Beth, and Amy, The Story of Their Lives, A Girls' Book was written by Louisa May Alcott and published in two parts. Roberts Brothers published the first part on September 30, 1868. After its success, with the first 2000 copies sold in just one month, the editor confirmed that Alcott should write a second part, which was published on April 14, 1869, and sold thirteen thousand copies in two weeks. The full book was edited and republished in 1880. It has never gone out of print. While generally read independently, *Little Women* was followed by two more novels in the series: *Little Men* in 1871 and *Jo's Boys* in 1886.

The book chronicles approximately fifteen years in the lives of four sisters and their close family and friends in Concord, Massachusetts. The book is largely autobiographical and fictionalizes the life of Alcott (Jo) and her three sisters: Anna (Meg); Lizzie (Beth); and May (Amy). Like their characters, Lizzie died at 23, weakened from scarlet fever, and May was quite artistic, making the original illustrations for the publication of *Little Women*. Alcott had already published several of the girls' stories and experiences in other, shorter pieces. In addition to drawing on her own life, Alcott makes allusions to other books throughout her novel, most explicitly *The Pilgrim's Progress*, a Christian allegory by John Bunyan published in 1684.

Alcott was asked to write *Little Women* in 1867 by the editor Thomas Niles, who wanted a girls' book. When Alcott started the book in May 1868, she wrote in her journal that, "I plod away, though I don't enjoy this sort of thing. Never liked girls or knew many, except my sisters; but our queer plays and experiences may prove interesting, though I doubt it." In writing a book for adolescents, Alcott decided to make the tone simple and direct, based on real experiences rather than sensationalized ones. Each part was written in approximately three months, sometimes a chapter a day, with very little rewriting or editing. Her editor Niles and Alcott herself found her first twelve chapters "dull." Both were surprised and pleased by the scale of its success.

Contemporary critics praised *Little Women* for being a well-written, lively, and enjoyable book for children and adults alike. *Little Women* differed from other books for girls at the time, such as Susan Warner's *The Wide, Wide World*, by giving depth to its female characters and avoiding being overly moralistic. Little Women is considered one of the great American novels and has been adapted several times as a radio show, play, opera, and film. The most recent film was made in 1994 and stars Susan Sarandon, Winona Ryder, Clare Danes, Kirsten Dunst, and Christian Bale.

Character List

Meg

Margaret is the oldest of the March sisters. In Book I, she hopes to conquer her vanity and do her work cheerfully. In Book II, she marries John Brooke and has twins, Daisy and Demi.

Jo

Josephine is the second oldest March sister. She is a writer and a tomboy. Jo is modeled after Louisa May Alcott herself. She famously cuts and sells her hair to help her sick father. Though best friends with Laurie, she eventually marries Professor Bhaer and opens a school for boys.

Beth

Elizabeth is the third eldest sister. She is a quiet, selfless, shy girl, who only wishes to be at home with her family. She loves music and plays the piano. In Book I, Beth gets scarlet fever, and recovers, though in Book II she dies.

Also the name of Laurie and Amy's daughter.

Amy

The youngest, Amy is the pet of the family. She loves art and is quite vain, but learns to be elegant, kind, and generous. Always planning to marry rich, she considers but rejects Fred Vaughn and marries Laurie.

Marmee

The girls' name for Margaret March, mother of Meg, Jo, Beth, and Amy.

Father

Mr. March is a philosopher and pastor. During the war, he serves as a chaplain for the Union Army. A good man, but very unworldly, he is modeled after Bronson Alcott, Louisa's father.

Hannah

The faithful servant and cook who is generally treated like a family member.

Hummels

The family of poor German immigrants who live near the Marches. On Christmas Day, the March girls give up their breakfast to this family. Beth gets scarlet fever from them.

Mr. Laurence or Grandfather

The March family's wealthy neighbor. He was good friends with Mrs. March's father, and becomes dear friends with all the Marches. He is especially close with Beth and gives her a piano.

Laurie

Theodore Lawrence, called Laurie by most or Teddy by Jo, is Mr. Laurence's nephew. He becomes a close friend and brother to the girls, particularly Jo. Without parents, he is largely influenced by the morals of the girls and their mother. After pining after Jo, but being refused, Laurie marries Amy.

Mr. Brooke

John Brooke is Laurie's tutor. He accompanies Mrs. March to Washington when Mr. March is sick, and he woos and marries Meg.

Scrabble

The rat in the garret where Jo writes.

Joanna

Beth's most cherished doll, who once belonged to Jo.

Aunt March

Great Aunt March is Mr. March's aunt. Rather old and cranky, she first has Jo as her companion, then Amy. She disapproves of how the girls are raised, but occasionally finds ways to be generous, funding Amy's trip abroad and leaving Plumfield to Jo when she dies.

King Family

The wealthy family Meg for whom Meg is a governess. Their family woes cause Meg to see that money cannot bring happiness.

Mr. Davis

The teacher at Amy's school. His corporal punishment of Amy for bringing pickled limes to school causes Mrs. March to withdraw her.

Mrs. Gardiner

Mother of Sallie. She invites Meg and Jo to a New Year's Ball.

Annie Moffat

A wealthy friend of Meg's, who invites Meg to stay for a fortnight with her.

Belle Moffat

Annie's sister, who dresses Meg up for the party at the end of the fortnight at Annie Moffat's.

Clara Moffat

Annie and Belle's eldest sister.

Sallie Gardiner

A wealthy friend of Meg's, of whose luxurious lifestyle Meg is very envious. At one point, she tempts Meg into buying silk for a dress, which she cannot afford. Sallie marries Ned Moffat.

Ned Moffat

Annie's brother who likes Meg and tries to dance and flirt with her. Marmee disapproves, and he marries Sallie Gardiner.

Major Lincoln

A gentleman at the Moffats' parties who says Meg's friends have made a fool and a doll of Meg when they dress her up.

Kate Vaughn

The eldest of four children who comes to visit Laurie. She is quite proper and looks down on the independent Americans.

Fred Vaughn

A rich friend of Laurie's. When he is young he cheats at croquet, but when he is older, he entertains Amy abroad, and she almost accepts his marriage proposal.

Frank Vaughn

Brother of Fred, with a lame leg due to an accident. Beth overcomes her bashfulness to talk to him out of pity.

Grace Vaughn

The youngest Vaughn, she and Amy get along well.

Lotty

One of the Hummel children, who helps Meg run errands when she is married.

Dr. Bangs

The doctor who treats Beth when she has scarlet fever.

Esther

Aunt March's maid. French and Catholic, Esther is kind to Amy during her stay, witnessing her will, practicing French, and setting up a chapel where Amy can pray.

Polly

Aunt March's terror of a parrot.

Kitty Bryant

Amy's best friend when she is young, whose ring she envies.

Miss Crocker

An elderly woman from town who gossips, so the girls call her "Croaker." She calls during Marmee's experiment leaving the girls to cook for themselves, to everyone's dismay.

Miss Randal

A girl Laurie likes for a while in college, about whom the girls tease him.

Flo or Florence

The girls' cousin, and Mary Carrol's daughter. Amy has to wear Flo's ugly hand-me-down clothes when she is young, but Amy enjoys traveling with Flo abroad.

Aunt Carrol

The girls' aunt, she invites Amy to travel overseas with her family.

Parker

One of Laurie's many college friends who pines after Amy.

Meg Chester

One of Amy's friends. Meg and Amy have a falling out at the art fair, but make up through Amy's kindness.

Mrs. Chester

Meg's mother, who rudely asks Amy to work another table at the art fair in order to favor her own daughter.

Daisy

Meg and John's daughter, actually named Margaret, a sweet-tempered angel.

Demi

Meg and John's don, actually named John but nicknamed "Demijohn" by Laurie, an inquisitive and mischievous boy.

Mrs. Kirke

One of Marmee's friends who runs a boarding house in New York. Jo goes to work for Mrs. Kirke and teach her daughters.

Kitty

Mrs. Kirke's daughter.

Minnie

Mrs. Kirke's daughter.

Mr. Dashwood

The editor of the Weekly Volcano where Jo anonymously submits sensation stories in New York.

Mr. Bhaer

Friedrich, or Fritz, is a German professor who tutors at the boardinghouse in New York. He befriends Jo, and eventually marries her.

Franz

Mr. Bhaer's nephew, whom he promised his sister he would care for.

Emil

Mr. Bhaer's nephew, whom he promised his sister he would care for.

Tina

The young daughter of the ironing woman at the boarding house, she is a great fan of Mr. Bhaer's.

Miss Norton

A young, rich woman at the boardinghouse who is kind to Jo and takes her to a literary symposium.

Teddy

Jo's name for Laurie, also the name of her youngest son.

Rob

Jo’s elder son, named for Jo’s father.

Major Themes

Family and Marriage

The dominant theme of Little Women, as for girls in the nineteenth century, is family. The characters are defined by their familial relations and behaviors toward each other, and all are deeply invested in cultivating and supporting one another.

Throughout the novel, Alcott emphasizes the importance of family as not only a practical or economic unit but also a deeply meaningful one. When Aunt March offers to adopt a child, Father and Mother reject, insisting that they stay together. Without money or an urge to be very active in society, much of the March family's experiences and emotions take place within the family unit, inventing plays and clubs. The main dramas play out within the family as well, such as Jo and Amy's fight over the burnt manuscript. The girls miss their Father or Mother not because it makes their work harder, but because they are the moral head and heart of the family.

The theme of family encompasses the girls marrying and starting families of their own. Marmee teachers her daughters that having a loving husband and family is the greatest joy a woman can have, as emphasized by the concluding line of the book. Marmee's discussions with the girls about their duties to each other and their parents evolve into discussions about their duties to their husbands and children. Alcott and her characters devote great attention to finding good husbands. Each of the grooms spends significant time meeting and being accepted by the family before the marriage. Laurie in particular evolves from being a neighbor and friend to being a son and brother. While Jo initially a threat to her family unit, the March family actually expands to include these new families. Thus, marriage does not replace but rather enhances the familial bond.

Poverty

Little Women focuses on a particular type of poverty – that of the working poor. Kindness is shown to those in the book with less than the March family, such as the Hummels. But as Amy and Laurie discuss, "out-and-out beggars get taken care of, but poor gentlefolks fare badly," including aspiring young men and women. The poverty of the March family is particularly touching because it is a result of Mr. Alcott's attempt to help a friend. Meg and Amy have to learn several times to live within their means, but all the girls come to believe that love is preferable to riches. Meg marries John Brooke, and Amy tells Laurie she would have married him even if he were a pauper. Time and again we are reminded – by the King family, the Gardiners, the Moffats, and Aunt March – that wealth is no guarantee of happiness. The Laurences show us that money can be usefully and helpfully employed, particularly to help others. Poverty, while challenging, can foster the development of creativity, strength, and character.

Work

Several characters throughout the novel learn that honest work, while not easy, is rewarding and worthwhile. Meg often resents her work, envying her friends' leisurely ways, but she strives to do her work more cheerfully, and is rewarded by her Father's recognition. John Brooke defends Meg and the working class to Kate Vaughn as an example of American independence. During vacation, when the girls experiment with resting from work, they grow idle and dissatisfied, and they learn from Marmee to maintain a balance of work and play. Again when their Father is sick, Marmee urges the girls to invest their energy into their work to keep their spirits up, led by Hannah who believes that "work is the panacea for most afflictions" (130). When they neglect their duties, Beth becomes ill.

Jo sees her writing as work that can help her achieve independence and support her family, but she learns an important lesson from Mr. Bhaer in keeping her work honest and focusing on the means and not just the ends of her efforts. In the end, Jo's happiness comes in working alongside Mr. Bhaer. Even Laurie, who dreads going into his grandfather's business for most of the book, also embraces working for his grandfather as a meaningful way of life, rather than pursuing music.

Morality and Society

There is a strong emphasis on morality throughout the book, particularly in contrast to what is considered proper or expected in society. In particular, the March family stresses duty and generosity.

For the Marches, morality is implicitly linked to their Christianity, as made clear by the allusions to Pilgrim's Progress and Mr. March's role as a minister, but also to their wishes for true happiness. Alcott describes how difficult it is for her characters to make moral decisions, but when they do, they are happier than when they make immoral ones. When the girls share their Christmas breakfast with the Hummels, they are happy with their choice and rewarded by a feast from Mr. Laurence. Laurie is thankful to Meg for making him promise to avoid drinking, and grateful that his promises to his grandfather and Marmee keep him out of mischief. The King family provides a counterexample of the unhappiness that comes to the family because of the son's immoral behavior. Amy is deeply grateful that she married Laurie for love, rather than marrying Fred Vaughn for money. Jo tries to weave morality through her sensation stories by making her "sinners repent," but when "morals didn't sell," she leaves the morals out. Mr. Bhaer teaches her, though, that meeting society's demand is not always worthwhile, and she feels very guilty about her immoral stories. After Beth dies, when Jo writes from the heart, she is rewarded by the return of Mr. Bhaer and her eventual marriage.

Independence and Women's Rights

Independence is a major theme of the book. Despite her devotion to her family, Jo craves independence through work, in order that she may support them. Laurie also struggles with his wish to be independent from his grandfather, feeling this is in conflict with his duty and love for his only family. The characters view their independence as part of their upbringing in America.

For many characters, independence is linked to women's rights implicitly through the book, particularly when it is considered in historical context. Compared to other girls' novels at the time, the female characters in *Little Women* are opinionated, well educated, and accomplished girls who are treated with great respect in their homes. Marmee encourages her girls to take an interest in current events. The limitations society places on them because they are girls are most strongly expressed by Jo. In addition to her wishes to run, skate, and ride as boys do, she is tempted to run away with Laurie to have adventures, but rejects the idea because she is a girl. Jo also insists on helping to contribute to the household as a condition of her marriage to Mr. Bhaer.

Self-Improvement

The story of the Meg, Jo, Beth, and Amy is one of constant change. The girls are always working to improve their characters, learn from their mistakes, and move closer to their ideal selves. This theme is made explicit in Part I, when the girls "play pilgrims" in order to address their personal character flaws while their Father is away. This effort does not end as they enter adulthood, but continues as they are confronted with new experiences. Meg learns to conquer vanity in her marriage with John, Jo struggles to accept her duty and develop into a woman, even Beth works to peacefully and cheerfully go to her death, and Amy strives to apply her experiences overseas to become generous and grateful. Marmee confides in Jo that she has struggled to contain her temper for forty years, and that the struggle may continue for another forty years. The girls' attempts to grow into "little women" are explicitly encouraged by their Mother and Father who explain that self-improvement is both possible and valuable. The goal of such improvement is not only entrance to Heaven, but also a more pleasant experience for themselves and others in their current lives.

Duty and Sacrifice

Duty is a common thread used to justify why the characters should make sacrifices and moral decisions. Even from a young age, the girls consider themselves having duties toward the household, and learn the consequences of shirking those duties. The girls also speak about their duties to society, to host callers and to make formal calls. Later, Marmee speaks to Meg about caring for her husband and her children in terms of her shared duty to both of them.

Duty is often considered in terms of self-sacrifice. Father and John Brooke serve in the army despite the love awaiting them at home and despite Father's age. Marmee considers her sacrifice minor compared to that of a man she meets who has given all his sons to the war. Laurie decides to follow his grandfather's wishes dutifully, giving up his castle in the air of pursuing music. Jo sacrifices her dream of being a great writer and accepts the duty of caring for Mother and Father after Beth dies, which she finds very difficult, but rewarding.

Selfless Generosity

Another aspect of morality emphasized throughout the book is that of generosity. This quality is prized from the very beginning of the book, when the girls decide to give Marmee presents instead of themselves, then share their Christmas breakfast with the Hummels. Beth is held up as the best example of selfless caring of others, unappreciated until she is gone. Even when Beth is dying, she still derives pleasure from making gifts for unknown schoolchildren passing outside her window. Amy strives to be more like Beth, explicitly battling selfishness as her burden. Her growth in this area is shown when she returns her art pieces to May Chester's table at the fair. Alcott portrays those who are generous with their wealth favorably, such as Mr. Laurence's gifts to the family and Laurie and Amy's generosities after they are married. On the other hand, Aunt March is considered sad in part because she only shares her blessings very selectively.

Literature and Language

Alcott imbues her characters with a love of language and text. Alcott exposes the reader to many forms of language, including German, French, Hannah's dialect, the individual voices of the characters in their letters, Jo's slang, and Alcott's own creative poetry and prose.

The characters' constant references and allusions to books indicate that they are well read and assume others to be so. The most explicit example of this is Alcott's structuring of Part I to mirror *Pilgrim's Progress.* Amy's misuse of words is playfully mocked, and when she is abroad, she regrets not having been more studious. A shared love of books brings Jo closer with the Laurences and with Mr. Bhaer. German literature in particular plays a role in both Meg's and Jo's courtship.

Glossary of Terms

"Lapse of lingy"
Amy means to say lapsus linguae, which is Latin for "slip of the tongue"

'Aisy
Without hardship; a dialectic shortening of "easy"

Abominable
Detestable, awful

Aristocratic
Belonging to a high social or political class; of the nobility

Assiduity
Persistent and diligent effort

Belladonna
A medicine made of deadly nightshade, used as a home remedy for scarlet fever

Benevolence
Inclination to do good and help others

Blancmange
Dessert similar to pudding made with cream and sugar and a thickener such as cornstarch

Capricious
Impulsive and fickle, likely to change based on chance rather than reason

Chaplain
A priest, pastor, or other clergy member assigned to an official group, such as a military unit

Conservatory
A greenhouse for growing flowers

Coquetry
Playful, flirtatious behavior intended to arouse interest

Cravat

Neckband; forerunner of the modern necktie

Droll
Comical in a whimsical manner

Dudgeon
Intense indignation

Ennui
Intense boredom and listlessness

Fashion-plate
A picture advertising the latest fashions

Governess
A woman employed to watch and teach children in a private home; a nanny

Indolent
Habitually lazy and procrastinating

Libel
A written insult

Out
In this context, being "out" means having officially entered into society. "Coming out" was sometimes celebrated with parties similar to a debutante ball.

Panacea
Cure-all

Penitent
Regretful

Propriety
Proper behavior; in the case of Mr. Brooke and Kate Vaughn to "play propriety" at Camp Laurence, this means chaperone

Tranquility
An untroubled and peaceful state

Truckle
Yield to out of weakness

Vortex

A fast-moving spiral, such as a whirlpool

Short Summary

Little Women chronicles approximately fifteen years in the life of the March family. It comes largely from the experiences of the family of the author Louisa May Alcott. The Marches live in Concord, Massachusetts, and the book begins at Christmas, 1861, during the Civil War. Part I of the book covers just over one year.

The March family is relatively poor, though they can still afford one servant and they often share whatever they have with others less fortunate. Mr. March is a philosopher and teacher. He serves as a Chaplain in the Union Army until he gets ill. After being nursed to health by his wife, he returns to Concord and becomes a minister. A kind but unworldly man, he lost the family property trying to help a friend, which brought poverty upon the family for some time. He leads the family quietly, urging Christian morality and kindness.

Mrs. March, or "Marmee" is a strong, kind, and moral character. She advocates a healthy balance of work and play and urges her daughters to marry good, kind men. She is patient with the family's poverty, reminding the girls to remember their many blessings. She is the rock of the family. When she leaves to help nurse her husband, she must later return to nurse her daughter Beth, and she comforts the girls through many challenges.

In Part I, the girls decide to improve their characters while their Father is gone, so they can make him proud when he returns. They use the story *Pilgrim's Progress* to add fun and meaning to their goals.

Meg, sixteen, wants to overcome vanity and complain less about poverty and hard work. She struggles with envying luxurious things, and occasionally tries them for herself, but always feels disingenuous and wrong. She chooses to marry the poor but good John Brooke, who tutored her neighbor Laurie. Meg and John are very happy together and have twins, Daisy and Demi.

Jo, fifteen at the start, is based on the author and is often considered the main character. She is a tomboy and a writer with a fierce temper and a dislike for doing what society thinks is proper. Jo struggles throughout the book to become womanlier. She is completely devoted to her family and tries to earn money writing so she can help them. Jo is best friends with the March family's neighbor Laurie, who eventually proposes to her, but she loves him only as a brother. After nursing her sister Beth through illness and death, Jo becomes tenderer, and marries a German professor named Mr. Bhaer. They open a school for boys.

Beth, thirteen at the start, is a quiet and selfless girl. She loves music and is given a piano by their neighbor Mr. Laurence. Beth struggles to overcome her bashfulness throughout Part I. She also contracts scarlet fever while helping a poor family. She comes very close to dying in Part I, and, forever weakened by the fever, dies in Part

II.

Amy, twelve, is the young spoiled pet of the family. She loves to draw and tries to use long words she does not understand in order to sound older and fancy. Similar to Meg, Amy has aristocratic tastes. She tries to be less selfish and become a true lady, generous and graceful. Amy is very much Jo's opposite, and Jo is heartbroken when an Aunt asks Amy to go abroad instead of tomboy Jo. Amy studies art abroad and considers marrying friend Fred Vaughn since he is rich, though she does not love him. Her conscience and their friend Laurie help her realize that would be a mistake. In Europe, Amy and Laurie fall in love and are married.

Laurie, the neighbor, is Jo's age. He is raised by his grandfather, who always fears Laurie will run away to play music rather than stay to work in the family business. Laurie benefits greatly from the March family's influence, and they benefit from his generosity. In addition to being wealthy, Laurie is kind, lively, and good. He is devastated when Jo does not accept his marriage proposal. His grandfather takes him overseas, where he realizes he loves Jo like a brother, and he falls in love with Amy.

From the interactions among these main characters, Alcott weaves a lively but domestic, and incredibly popular tale of American youth in the nineteenth century. Her characters focus on their moral development but they have weaknesses and humor to make them human and relatable. Alcott's deep depiction of the female characters was unique for its time and implicitly argued for women's equality in the home and outside of it. Through their experiences, the characters learn to appreciate the enduring importance of family, the happiness derived from being selfless and dutiful, the disconnection between wealth and happiness, and the benefits of working hard to improve oneself and one's home.

Quotes and Analysis

"I think there were not in all the city four merrier people than the hungry little girls who gave away their breakfasts and contented themselves with bread and milk that Christmas morning. 'That's loving our neighbor better than ourselves, and I like it,' said Meg..."

Narrator, 16

The themes of generosity and self-sacrifice are introduced very early in the novel, with the girls giving up their Christmas breakfast for their neighbors. The act of giving brings the girls joy. Meg's allusion to the Golden Rule has two effects: it frames their actions in terms of Christianity and is a play on words, since the Hummels are in fact the March's neighbors. This quote thus illustrates the girls' love of language and how Alcott uses small, domestic stories as parables for greater moral questions.

"Don't laugh at the spinsters, dear girls, for often very tender, tragic romances are hidden away in the hearts that beat so quietly under the sober gowns, and many silent sacrifices of youth, health, ambition, love itself, make the faded faces beautiful in God's sight."

Narrator, 402

Alcott herself is a determined spinster, and here asks her readers for sympathy and defends the choices of those like her. Alcott's life, like Jo's was full of sacrifice and hard work so that she could support her family. In the historical context of nineteenth century England, having received letters from countless readers after Part I wondering only about the marital fates of her characters, and in a book where she describes marriage as "the sweetest chapter in the romance of womanhood" (232), Alcott here defends an alternate path.

"...I shall never stop loving you; but the love is altered, and I have learned to see that it is better as it is. Amy and you changed places in my heart, that's all. I think it was meant to be so, and would have come about naturally, if I had waited, as you tried to make me; but I never could be patient, and so I got a heartache. I was a boy then, headstrong and violent; and it took a hard lesson to show me my mistake. For it was one, Jo, as you said, and I found it out, after making a fool of myself..."

Laurie to Jo, 406

This passage is one of several justifications to Alcott's readers for Laurie not marrying Jo. After Part I was published, Alcott's readers wrote to her begging for Jo and Laurie to marry. Alcott had to convince them that Laurie marrying Amy was both believable and desirable. Marmee's disapproval of Laurie's match with Jo and her approval of Laurie's match with Amy strengthens Alcott's argument. Alcott also foreshadows both Amy and Laurie's engagement and Jo's acceptance of it several times.

This quote also serves to mark Laurie's awareness of his transition from boyhood to manhood. In Europe, Laurie let go of both his boyhood dreams – marrying Jo and being a famous musician, and he returns as a man.

"There is a demand for whisky, but I think you and I do not care to sell it. If the respectable people knew what harm they did, they would not feel the living was honest. They haf no right to put poison in the sugarplum, and let the small ones eat it. No, they should think a little, and sweep mud in the street before they do this thing."

Professor Bhaer to Jo, 326

With this statement, Professor Bhaer awakens Jo to what she tried to deny - that the means of her work were as important as the ends. Jo is arguing that "many very respectable people make an honest living" writing sensation stories. Alcott, liked Jo, published sensation stories, but under a pseudonym. Professor Bhaer helps Jo see that her living is not honest. Much as Jo teased Amy for being mercenary, Jo too was pursuing money at the cost of her moral judgment. This encounter not only helps Jo return to her morality but also deepens her admiration of her friend.

This statement goes beyond Jo to chastise all those who earn a living off harmful products. Alcott and the March family believe in temperance, not drinking alcohol, so the example of whisky is an apt one.

"I've been trying to cure it for forty years, and have only succeeded in controlling it. I am angry nearly every day of my life, Jo, but I have learned not to show it; and I still hope to learn not to feel it, though it may take me another forty years to do so."

Marmee to Jo, 75

Marmee confides that, like Jo, she has a strong temper. This surprises Jo and the reader, given Marmee's role in the book. Marmee sharing this secret with Jo demonstrates that Jo is moving toward adulthood. The statement also signifies the characters' lifetime commitment to improving themselves. While their morality is rooted in Christianity, Marmee's best inspiration is the people around her, particularly being a good example for her daughters. This confirms the importance of family to the Marches.

Marmee's everyday anger is not explained, although Marmee confirms that she gets angry when "Aunt March scolds, or people worry" her. Given Marmee's other characteristics, it is likely that poverty, injustice, and immorality are the main causes of her anger.

"Money is a needful and precious thing--and, when well used, a noble thing--but I never want you to think it is the first or only prize to strive for. I'd rather see you poor men's wives, if you were happy, beloved, contented, than queens on thrones, without self-respect or peace."

Marmee to Meg and Jo, 92

This quote encapsulates the March family's approach to the relationship between happiness and wealth. This contradicts the view of society, as represented by Aunt March and Mrs. Moffat, who believe that pretty Meg should marry rich for the good of her family.

Despite this early lesson, Meg and Jo continue to struggle with their views on poverty. Meg chooses to marry John Brooke, and she makes a few mistakes before learning to be contented. Jo sacrifices her morals writing for money, but end up marrying the man who helped her stop, despite his great poverty. Amy even tells Laurie she wishes he were poor, so she could demonstrate her love by choosing him anyway.

In addition, the Laurences often make their money "a noble thing" through its good use.

"I only did as I'd be done by. You laugh at me when I say I want to be a lady, but I mean a true gentlewoman in mind and manners, and I try to do it as far as I know how. I can't explain exactly, but I want to be above the little meannesses and follies and faults that spoil so many women. I'm far from it now, but I do my best, and hope in time to be what Mother is."

Amy to Jo and Beth, 284

This quote demonstrates the development of Amy's character. After her forgiveness of the Chesters' meanness at the art fair, and her generosity in returning her pieces to May's table, Amy feels satisfied in knowing she has acted properly - not only in accordance with society, but also in accordance with what is moral. Amy in this sense reconciles the conflict between morality and society with which other characters struggle. Amy's wish to be like Mother, who is kind and has a few aristocratic tastes, but is not fashionable, demonstrates her focus on shaping her character rather than just her appearance, as Marmee bade her do after the pickled lime incident.

Here Amy also gains Jo's respect, and Jo hopes that Amy will be rewarded for her good deeds, which Amy is with a trip abroad, to Jo's dismay.

"Boys are trying enough to human patience, goodness knows, but girls are infinitely more so, especially to nervous gentleman with tyrannical tempers and no more talent for teaching than Dr. Blimber. Mr. Davis knew any quantity of Greek, Latin, algebra, and olgies of all sorts so he was called a fine teacher, and manners, morals, feelings, and examples were not considered of any particular importance."

Narrator, 64

This description of Amy's schoolteacher undermines his teaching style and the corporal punishment he is about to issue Amy. Louisa May Alcott's schoolteacher was an educator who had strong yet unconventional ideas about educating the entire child - including "manners, morals, feelings, and examples" rather than just focusing on rote knowledge. These ideas took time to gain credibility, to the financial detriment of the March family, but later became very influential in pedagogical philosophy. Later in *Little Women* and particularly in *Little Men*, Mr. Bhaer and Jo later apply the whole student approach at their school for boys.

"I'll try and be what he loves to call me, 'a little woman,' and not be rough and wild, but do my duty here instead of wanting to be somewhere else."

Jo, to Marmee, Meg, Beth, and Amy, 10

Herein lies Jo's pronounced goal, at the very beginning of the book, the conflict which will drive her development. Prior to hearing Father's letter, Jo announced her wish to join the army and fight with her Father. She dreams of doing something splendid and traveling abroad, and she is tempted to run away with Laurie when he proposes it. Jo is also sorely disappointed when Amy is asked to go overseas instead of her. Beth is thankful that Jo will not travel so far away. It is through nursing Beth that Jo learns to accept her sacrifice and make her peace with being at home. Beth asks Jo to take her places and reassures her that she will be "happier in doing that than writing splendid books or seeing all the world."

For Jo, doing her duty is intrinsically caught up in being a woman, whereas adventures are related to being boyish. Thus, she resists some aspects of womanhood, feeling that they will constrain her. Thus, it is only after she gives up her dreams of adventure at Beth's request and accepts her duty at home that she is open to marriage, considered in the book as the pinnacle of a woman's joy. In Jo's case, instead of being one of the boys, she transforms her duty into caring for them.

"Amy's lecture did Laurie good, though, of course, he did not own it till long afterward; men seldom do, for when women are the advisers, the lords of creation don't take advice till they have persuaded themselves that it is just what they intended to do; then they act upon it, and, if it succeeds, they give the weaker vessel half the credit of it; if it fails, they generously give her the whole."

Narrator, 384

Alcott's direct engagement with her reader throughout the book gives her work a conversational tone. In this case, using Laurie as her example, Alcott implies inequity in gender relations. Her use of the terms "lords of creation," "weaker vessel," and "generously" are clearly sarcastic. The purpose of this technique is two-fold. By discussing Laurie's situation obliquely, she gives us insight into his thought process that is informative for understanding the book. However, she also enjoys a laugh at men and makes a political statement for her readers. Given that her book was written for girls, this likely had an effect of solidarity building.

Later, Laurie's acknowledgment to Jo that Amy's lecture did do him good makes him all the more exceptional as a man.

Summary and Analysis of Chapter 1 through Chapter 5

Summary

Chapter 1 Playing Pilgrims

The story begins on Christmas Eve, where the four daughters are gathered in their simple living room lamenting that, this year, they are too poor to have presents on Christmas.

Meg is sixteen and quite pretty. She can be vain, especially about her soft, white hands. Jo is fifteen years old, a tomboy with a fierce temper. Jo loves to write stories and plays, which the girls act out. Beth is thirteen and exceptionally quiet, but she loves music and her family. Beth loves music and her family. Amy is the youngest at twelve. She is vain about her appearance and tries to act like a lady, using long words incorrectly. She enjoys drawing and longs to be a famous artist.

Each of the girls only has one dollar, and their mother feels that spending money on presents is wasteful during wartime. To cheer themselves up, the girls decide they will each buy themselves a present. Meg wants nice things, Jo wants a book, Beth new music, and Amy drawing pencils.

But as they prepare for their mother's arrival, they decide that instead of buying presents for themselves, they will all buy presents for their Mother, "Marmee." When Marmee comes in, they enjoy a simple supper, and sit together by the fire to read a cherished letter from their Father. Mr. March, a philosopher, teacher, and pastor, was too old to be a soldier in the Union Army, so he joined as a chaplain. The whole family misses him dearly and worries about his safety. Father's letter reminds them to be dutiful, loving and kind, so when he returns he "may be fonder and prouder than ever of my little women."

Inspired by the letter, the girls decide to play a game based on *Pilgrim's Progress* and each work toward improving a personal character flaw. Meg's goal is to be less vain and do her work dutifully without complaint. Jo hopes to be womanlier and less wild. Beth aims to be less bashful and happy with her work, not envying girls with nice pianos. Amy vows to be less selfish. Marmee promises to give them guidebooks and loving support for their journeys. Everyone sings together and then goes to bed.

Chapter 2 A Very Merry Christmas

The girls wake up to find books under their pillows, with an inscription in each from their mother, and decide to read their books every morning. Inspired by the book, Amy acts on her wish to be less selfish by spending all her money on a large bottle of cologne for her mother, rather than saving some money for herself. The girls hide their presents.

Marmee returns and asks the girls if they will send their Christmas breakfast to the nearby family of immigrants, where a single, sick mother lives with six children without food or firewood. Despite their hunger, the girls agree, and they all walk over to the Hummel family's home and spend the morning sharing their food and kindness. The Hummel children call the girls "angels," and the girls are deeply happy to have "loved our neighbor better than ourselves."

Upon returning home, the girls surprise their mother with their gifts, who is very touched. They then prepare their Christmas play, written by Jo, and performed for twelve of their friends. Jo plays the male parts, and there are a few accidents, as all the props and sets are made by hand. The play is a great success, and afterwards the girls and audience are surprised by a luxurious and fancy feast. Mr. Laurence, the wealthy gentleman who lives next door, heard about the girls giving up their Christmas breakfast to the poor Hummels, and sent the elaborate supper as a reward. Mr. Laurence is perceived as proud, but the girls are curious about his bashful nephew.

Chapter 3 The Laurence Boy

Meg and Jo are invited to a New Year's Eve dance at the Gardiner house. While getting ready, it is quickly apparent that tomboy Jo is ill suited for such a party, with a dress burnt from standing too close to the fire, gloves stained with lemonade, and little sense of proper, ladylike ways to behave. While trying to curl Meg's hair, Jo accidentally burns off the hair instead. Meg is much more ladylike, despite having to share her gloves with Jo, not having a silk dress and wearing very tight shoes. Meg tells Jo that she will raise her eyebrows if Jo is acting improperly.

At the party, unable to dance because of her burnt dress, Jo stumbles into a corner where Theodore Laurence, nephew of their wealth neighbor, is also hiding. The boy, called Laurie, is fifteen like Jo, and he is quickly drawn out of his shyness by her boyish nature, and the two get along very well.

Meg beckons Jo away saying she sprained her ankle in her tight, high-heeled shoes. Jo tries to get coffee and ice for Meg, but spills the coffee down her dress. Laurie helps Jo and entertains them both, then offers a ride home in his carriage. While Jo is reluctant to accept a favor, Laurie insists. Meg reflects that it is nice to sometimes feel elegant like a lady, but Jo points out that their family is just as happy as elegant people with fine things.

Chapter 4 Burdens

Everyone is grumpy on returning to the first day of work after the holidays. Meg is particularly frustrated that some people enjoy restful days and nice parties all the time, while she must work because she is poor. Meg remembers when her family had more wealth and comforts, before Mr. March lost his property trying to help a friend. When that happened, Meg and Jo both asked their parents to let them work.

As a governess for the wealthy King family, Meg daily sees all the luxuries she longs for and struggles to stay content. Jo works as a companion for her cranky Great Aunt March, reading to her and helping with small chores. She enjoys stealing away to Aunt March's library when she can. Beth, too shy for school, spends her days at home working tirelessly to help Hannah, caring for her dolls and cats with deep tenderness, and quietly pining for a nice piano. The narrator points out that we often take the Beths in the world for granted, quietly making our lives lovely, until they are gone. Amy is a pretty favorite among her classmates, and, like Meg, she longs to be an elegant, aristocratic lady. She looks up to and confides in Meg, and Jo has a special friendship with Beth. She laments her flat nose and the used, ugly clothes she inherits from her cousin Florence.

At the end of the day, the girls relate stories. Jo tells how Aunt March chastised her for reading rubbish while Aunt March slept, but allowed Jo to read her the story, and enjoyed it despite herself. Jo laments that Aunt March has chosen to have a life devoid of enjoyable things, despite being rich. Meg describes how an elder son of the King family disgraced his house by gambling, and she is grateful that her family acts properly and loves each other. Amy describes a friend at school whose nice ring she envied, until the friend got into trouble and was humiliated, and Amy no longer envied her. Beth recounts seeing their neighbor Mr. Laurence hook a fish on his cane and give it to a woman at the market who was trying to work in return for food. Lastly, Marmee describes meeting a man at the Soldier's Aid Society whose four sons had all gone to war yet he was cheerful and proud. Marmee felt bad for missing Father and gave the man a nice bundle and some money, thanking him for reminding her to be grateful and sacrifice willingly for the good cause.

At Jo's request, Marmee tells another story, of four girls who were safe and comfortable, yet discontented. They meet an old woman who tells them that to be contented, they must remember their blessings. This works, for one girl finds that wealth cannot keep sorrow out of families, another that youth and spirit are greater blessings than riches, another that begging would be even harder than errands, and the last that character is better than nice rings. Seeing this, the girls vow to complain less and work to deserve the blessings they have.

Chapter 5 Being Neighborly

One day Jo, intent on getting to know Laurie, throws a snowball at Laurie's window. She learns that he has had a bad cold and is bored. He invites her over, and the girls all send gifts with Jo, including Beth's cats, which make Laurie laugh and forget his shyness. Jo learns that Laurie, in his loneliness, often watches their family's warm and loving activities, and she invites him to come visit. Jo tells stories about her family, and Laurie shows Jo their remarkable library, where she waits when Laurie goes to see the doctor.

Looking at a portrait of Mr. Laurence, Jo muses to herself that he looks kind, but strong-willed, and that she should not be afraid of him. Jo is startled by Mr. Laurence, who had quietly come in the room and heard all she said. He compliments Jo's grandfather, whom he knew well, and Jo remarks that she thinks Laurie needs more company. Over tea, seeing Jo and Laurie get along, Mr. Laurence comes to agree that Laurie should spend more time with the March family. After playing the piano for Jo, which upsets Mr. Laurence, Laurie sends her away with thanks for the present her mother sent and promises to visit soon.

Jo arrives home and describes the luxurious house and its inhabitants to her family. She learns from Marmee that Mr. Laurence's son married an Italian musician, despite his disapproval. When Laurie's parents died Mr. Laurence adopted him, but Laurie's talent for music reminds Mr. Laurence of his son, and makes him fear losing Laurie. Meg compliments Laurie's manners. Jo hopes that they will all be great friends, and Mrs. March agrees. Beth remarks that, just as in *Pilgrim's Progress*, they have found a Palace Beautiful – but first they must make it past the lions.

Analysis

These chapters lay the foundation for the rest of Part I. Chapter 1 introduces the main storyline of Part I, the girls' effort to improve their characters. The Christmas gifts that they wish for not only provide insight into the girls' personalities, but also become rewards for their individual quests: at the end of Part I, each girl will receive a Christmas present very similar to the one she wished for in Chapter 1.

Many of the major themes are introduced in these chapters, as well as the primary conflicts the characters will undergo. The story opens on the family unit, just as it will close in Part I and Part II, emphasizing the fundamental nature of family. The girls are complaining about their poverty, but find comfort in generously sacrificing their Christmas breakfast for the Hummels. This sacrifice not only feels personally rewarding, but is also in accordance with their Christian morality. They girls dedicate themselves to further self-improvement, with assistance and support from Mother, Father, and their guidebooks.

Alcott uses various techniques to foreshadow the conflicts her characters will undergo. Meg twists her ankle because of her vanity, wearing high-heeled shoes that are too small. Jo is ignorant of Laurie's compliment of her and hopes they should all be friends. Beth is introduced by the narrator with a lament that so many girls like her are underappreciated until they are gone. Amy shares the misfortunes of her friend getting in trouble at school, not foreseeing her own downfall. We even see Laurie's conflict with his grandfather around music.

Alcott's writing engages her readers in dialogue. Her narration is conversational, and she speaks to her readers directly. For example, she acknowledges, "Young readers like to know 'how people look.'" She will continue this style throughout the book, closing Part I by inviting feedback on its reception. Indeed, Alcott's decisions for Part II were partly influenced by the letters she received from readers asking her for specific endings.

Alcott is not only in dialogue with her readers, but also with other literature. Alcott weaves her own writings through the story. The play the girls perform is modeled on "Norna; or, The Witch's Curse," published posthumously in 1893 in *Comic Tragedies*. Her characters are often reading or referring to contemporary and classic books, such as the *Undine and Sintram* and the *Heir of Radclyffe* and *Arabian Nights*. These books suggest character traits, such as the family's experience with poverty in *The Vicar of Wakefield*, opposition to slavery in *Uncle Tom's Cabin*, Jo's sense of adventure in *Arabian Nights*, Meg's sense of romance in *Ivanhoe*, and Aunt March's worldview in William Belsham's *Essays, Philosophical, Historical, and Literary*.

The most explicit allusion in Alcott's text is her use of John Bunyan's *The Pilgrim's Progress*. The only Preface is an excerpt from the book, intended to "give some clue to the plan of the story." By applying this allegory of salvation to her girls, Alcott imbues their domestic struggles with a sense of heroic importance. Scholars debate whether the guidebook Marmee gives her girls is *Pilgrim's Progress* or *The New Testament*. Either way, the girls' journeys are clearly placed in a Christian context.

Summary and Analysis of Chapter 6 through Chapter 9

Summary

Chapter 6 Beth Finds the Palace Beautiful

One of the lions to get past before the Marches can enjoy the Palace Beautiful is their awkwardness because they are poor and the Laurences are wealthy. However, they soon learn that Laurie feels himself the benefactor, and they accept the mutual benefit. The March family's philosophy and hard work influences Laurie, and everyone enjoys the Laurence home except Beth, who cannot overcome her fear of the gruff Mr. Laurence. Mr. Laurence hears of this, and asks Mrs. March, so Beth can hear, if one of the girls could come over and play the piano to keep it in tune. Beth approaches him, and Mr. Laurence kindly tells her she reminds him of his own granddaughter. The next day Beth gathers her courage to go to the big house, where she finds easy music on the piano, and then returns daily.

To thank Mr. Laurence, Beth makes him a pair of slippers. In return, Mr. Laurence surprises Beth by giving her the cabinet piano that his granddaughter used to play. Beth is so moved that she decides to go thank Mr. Laurence in person, before she becomes too afraid. Mr. Laurence pulls her onto his knee and, remembering his lost granddaughter, Beth kisses him, and the two become fast friends.

Chapter 7 Amy's Valley of Humiliation

Amy sighs for money, wishing she could buy pickled limes to treat her friends at school. Meg gives her a quarter, and Amy brings the limes to school. One unkind girl reports the limes to Mr. Davis, the teacher.

Mr. Davis makes Amy throw the limes into the snow, then strikes her palm and makes her stand in front of the class until lunch. For Amy, the experience is deeply humiliating, since Amy's parents had never hit her. At recess, Amy takes her possessions and goes straight home. Marmee withdraws Amy from the school, but she lectures Amy on breaking the rules, and encourages her to be more modest. Amy, upon reflection, realizes that Laurie is accomplished, but not conceited, so people enjoy his natural charm.

Chapter 8 Jo Meets Apollyon

Laurie invites Jo and Meg to the theater, and Amy begs to go along, but Jo refuses. To get revenge, Amy burns up a book manuscript, a collection of stories that Jo had been writing for several years. Jo, who has a hot temper, shakes Amy and boxes her ears. Gradually Amy realizes she was wrong, but Jo will not forgive her. The next day Jo goes skating with Laurie. Amy follows, but Jo does not tell her which ice is safe, and Amy falls through the ice. Laurie rescues Amy, with Jo's help. At home, with Amy safe, Jo confesses to her Mother that she was consumed by anger and could have lost Amy as a result. Marmee then tells Jo that she, too, once had a very bad temper, but that she has learned to control it. Jo's Father has been a great help to her, and she tries to be an example for her girls. Jo takes great comfort and inspiration from her Mother sharing this weakness, and prays that she will never again let her anger bring her so close to tragedy.

Chapter 9 Meg Goes to Vanity Fair

In the spring, Meg goes to stay a fortnight with Annie Moffat. Mrs. March is concerned that Meg will return discontented, but consents to the trip. Meg is upset she does not have very nice things to take, but she remembers to be happy that she has this chance.

Meg is at first daunted by the luxurious environs, but she enjoys idling and dining finely, and begins to adopt the mannerisms of her hosts and envy her friends. When preparing for the first, smaller party, Meg is embarrassed by her second-best dress, and wears her nicest one, but it is still plain. She feels upset until she receives flowers from Laurie and a note from her mother. Rejuvenated, she shares the flowers with her friends and enjoys the party and a few honest compliments. Unfortunately, the party is spoiled for her by overhearing gossip that Meg's mother wants her to marry Laurie for his wealth, and that her friends hope Meg would tear her dress, so they can offer her another, nicer one for the next ball. Meg's pride is insulted, but she holds her tongue, and cries that night feeling that her innocent world has been corrupted by romantic speculation and gossip.

The next morning, the other girls show Meg more respect, thinking Laurie is courting her, which makes her laugh. Belle then kindly offers Meg a different dress for the next party, and asks to dress her up like Cinderella. Meg accepts, and the night of the party, she wears all the latest fashions, which brings her the attentions of high-society people. Meg enjoys the attention, but feels queer and uncomfortable. Laurie appears and is also uncomfortable, and tells Meg honestly that he does not like how she looks or is acting. Meg realizes she has been foolish, and Laurie apologizes for his rudeness. Meg spends the rest of the evening acting the part, dancing with Ned Moffat, flirting, and drinking champagne, despite not truly enjoying herself. She is quite ready to return home when the time comes.

At home, Meg confesses to Marmee and Jo. Mrs. March insists that they forget the gossip, and regrets sending Meg, but Meg is thankful, and admits that it is sometimes nice to be admired. Marmee says she understands, and that she hopes Meg will value the praise of those she respects, and be as modest as she is pretty. She explains that her plans for her girls are different than other mothers' – rather than hoping her daughters marry rich, she hopes they become good women and find true and loving husbands with whom to share duties and joys. She hopes they will prepare for that time by making their current home happy, and trust that good, sincere men will not be daunted by poverty.

Analysis

This section draws most heavily on *Pilgrim's Progress*, with each of the girls facing a challenge similar to that faced by Christian in the book. Beth must pass the lions, her fear of Mr. Laurence. For Christian, this is a test of faith, for in fact the lions are chained. Beth's faith in the kindness of the Laurences, her gratitude, and her pity for Mr. Laurence losing his granddaughter help her overcome her burden of bashfulness. When going into the Valley of Humiliation, Christian slips a little along the way, despite the help of Discretion, Piety, Charity, and Prudence. Amy's burden is selfishness, and her purchase of the limes is a selfish and indulgent "slip." While Marmee condemns the corporal punishment, she agrees that Amy needed the lesson, which Amy learns.

Like Christian, Jo meets Apollyon, a monster who tries to destroy him. The allusion serves to emphasize how evil Jo's temper is and likens it to an external demon she must defeat. Marmee urges Jo to use her faith in God to defeat her temper, as Christian defeats the monster. Like Christian, Meg passes through Vanity Fair, a fair devised to tempt passers-by into all indulging in the lusts of their heart. Also like Christian, Meg's dress is different from that of the other girls. While Christian ultimately escapes unscathed, Meg is tempted, but learns that her vanities cannot be indulged without consequences. Alcott uses simile to compare Meg to a jackdaw, who in Aesop's fable borrows fancy feathers to try being selected as king of the birds, but then is exposed as a fraud.

Poverty is a dominant theme in this section of the book. The difference in their wealth is initially a barrier to friendship with the Laurences, but as both parties are noble, they overcome that divide. Marmee later tells Meg and Jo, "Money is a needful and a precious thing,--and, when well used, a noble thing,--but I never want you to think it is the first or only prize to strive for." Both Amy and Meg struggle to accept living genuinely within their means, but cannot resist the attention that comes with luxuries like limes or silk dresses. Like the jackdaw in Aesop's fable, both are humiliated. The pressures and expectations of society differ from the morality espoused by the March family. Indeed, Alcott references Marmee reading Maria Edgeworth to the girls, whose popular story "The Purple Jar" urged the sensible choice of useful rather than pretty items.

In this chapter, we also see Meg concerned about poverty's affect on her marital prospects. The gossip at the party spoils her innocence and marks the beginning of Meg's transition from childhood to adulthood, to Jo's dismay. Marmee recognizes that the "time has come" to discuss her plans for marriage with her daughters. Marmee's description contradicts the dominant view of women's roles at the time, for though she describes marriage with a good man as "the best and sweetest thing which can happen to a woman," she also urges the girls not to marry for riches, or to demean themselves in aspiring for this goal.

Marmee embodies her wish for her girls not to fear marriage with a poor but loving man. She misses him, but takes comfort in knowing she is doing her duty to him and to her country, as well as in her Heavenly Father. This quick transition from discussing Father to discussing God, along with Father's absence and gentle encouragement from afar, draws easy comparisons between the two. Father, as a chaplain and minister, is a distant source of Christian comfort for the girls, and he inspires them to be good. The comparison also reflects on Alcott's portrayal of God, as similar to the kind of loving Father the girls know.

Summary and Analysis of Chapter 10 through Chapter 14

Summary

Chapter 10 The P.C. and P.O.

In the spring, the girls tend to their garden plots and form a secret society named the Pickwick Club, after Dickens, with each dressing and acting like a particular character. They create a weekly newspaper, which the narrator assures the readers is a copy of a genuine newspaper composed by four real girls. Jo proposes adding Laurie to the club, and Meg and Amy at first oppose, wanting to be private, but Beth speaks on Laurie's behalf and wins the day. Jo then shocks the club by revealing that Laurie was hiding in the closet all along. Laurie apologizes for the trick, and makes amends with the presentation of a post office, a converted birdhouse to sit in the hedge between the two houses. Delighted with the gift, the club enjoys a lively discussion and benefits from Laurie's presence. The post office, the narrator tells us, flourishes as well, passing trinkets and tickets as well as even a few love letters in the future.

Chapter 11 Experiments

In the summer, Meg and Jo celebrate that their employers are off for three months elsewhere, so they have vacation. The girls decide that after their hard work, they want to spend their days in idle enjoyment. Amy and Beth wish to have a rest as well, and Marmee grants permission for a one-week experiment, warning that they will miss the balance of some work and some play. The girls indulge in their activities, Meg buying and fixing up clothes new clothes, Jo reading to her heart's delight, Beth arranging her closet and learning music, and Amy drawing. They find the days growing longer and more tiring and pervaded with ennui. Marmee and Hannah make up for their housework, until the weekend, when Marmee gives Hannah a vacation and spends the day resting and going out.

The girls are relieved to have some work to do, but are surprised by how challenging the housework is. Meg spoils breakfast and Jo says she will make dinner and invites Laurie. Jo attempts to manage the kitchen, but ends up with burnt bread, salty strawberries, sour cream, meager lobster, and lumpy blancmange. In addition to Laurie, Miss Crocker, an elderly neighborhood gossip, calls for dinner and experiences the entire mess. Despite Jo's disappointment, they all enjoy a laugh over the meal, followed by a somber funeral for Pip, Beth's bird who was not fed all week. The girls continue to work into the evening, cleaning up and managing tea, and feel exhausted when Marmee returns.

Marmee asks if the girls enjoyed their experiment, and explains that she deliberately went away so they could see the effects of everyone deciding to be idle, rather than each doing her own duty. Work, she explains, helps everyone feel independent and useful, and it is important to balance work with time for pleasure. The girls each pledge to spend their summers learning a useful skill or accomplishment.

Chapter 12 Camp Laurence

Beth's delivery of the post one summer day brings several things. Meg receives one glove and a poem translated from German by Mr. Brooke, which makes Mrs. March wonder about Mr. Brooke's intentions for Meg. Jo receives a note from her Mother admiring how she is working to master her temper, for which she is grateful. Finally, Laurie has sent an invitation for all the girls to spend the day boating and camping with some visiting friends from England, along with a large-brimmed hat. Beth promises to come, despite her shyness, and the girls prepare for the day, Jo wearing her floppy hat against Meg's wishes.

The Vaughns, Kate, Fred, Frank, and Grace, are friendly though distinctly British. Kate is standoffish, Fred is a prankster, Frank is lame, and Grace gets on with Amy quite well. Ned Moffat also comes, wanting to see Meg, as does Mr. Brooke, Laurie's tutor, and Sallie Gardiner. Laurie's servants and housemen set up a great tent with food and games, and the party boats up the river and plays croquet. Both teams play well, teasing each other about Yankees and 1776, and Jo wins, despite Fred Vaughn cheating. Jo sees him and works very hard to control her temper, for which Meg and Laurie commend her. They help prepare lunch, then sit and play games. They begin with Rig-marole, a storytelling game, with Mr. Brooke starting a story about a young knight hoping for the hand of a poor princess, then the next person in line taking the story in a different direction, and so on. The next game is Truth, whereby Laurie and Jo make Fred confess that he cheated at croquet and that he thinks the English nation is perfect. While the others play Authors, Kate, Meg, and Mr. Brooke speak. Kate looks down on Meg for being a governess, but Mr. Brooke defends the independence of working men and women in America, and helps Meg read a German poem. It appears that Mr. Brooke is quite fond of Meg, but she has no idea. Ned Moffat makes his intentions more clear, but Meg avoids flirting, having learned from the gossip at the Moffats' party.

Chapter 13 Castles in the Air

After a frustrating day, Laurie spies the March girls going on a picnic and decides to follow them. He finds them in a clearing, and is given permission to join as long as he is not idle. The girls explain that as part of their *Pilgrim's Progress* game, they have been working on their goals over the vacation. In order to be outdoors, they come to this clearing, which they call Delectable Mountain, carrying poles and bags, and continue their work while looking out over the landscape. They discuss Heaven, and then each describes her or his favorite Castle in the Air, or dream for the future. Laurie wishes to be a famous musician in Germany. Meg wishes a nice home full of luxurious things and kind people. Jo wishes to write books, be famous, and have a stable of Arabian steeds. Amy wishes to go to Rome and be the most famous artist in the world, and Beth wishes just to stay at home with her family.

Laurie is afraid his grandfather will force him to go into business, despite Laurie's wishes, and says he would run away if there were anyone else to stay with grandfather. Jo encourages him for a moment, but Meg reminds him to be dutiful toward his grandfather and trust that he will be just and kind, as he has been with Mr. Brooke. Meg then describes what she heard from Mr. Laurence about Mr. Brooke, that he had given up better paying jobs to take care of his mother and now takes care of another elderly woman. That evening, listening to Beth play for Mr. Laurence, Laurie decides to stay with his grandfather and give up his 'castle' of being a musician.

Chapter 14 Secrets

Jo finishes a manuscript and then goes into town on a mysterious errand. Laurie sees her from a gymnasium, which Jo mistakes for a billiard saloon and chastises him. Laurie says he only goes to saloons occasionally, but Jo warns him to be careful not to get too wild, or Mother will prevent him visiting, as she does other fashionable gentlemen like Ned Moffat. After the lecture, Laurie and Jo agree to exchange secrets. Jo has left two stories with a newspaperman, and is waiting to see if he will print them, and Laurie encourages her.

Laurie's secret is that John Brooke has one of Meg's gloves, which is why only one was returned in Chapter 12. Laurie thinks the budding romance is quite lovely, but Jo feels upset and confused. To make her feel better, Laurie convinces her to run down the hill with him, like a boy. Jo gives in, and feels better, but Meg comes along and chastises her for romping. Jo defends herself, never wishing to grow old, feeling already that Meg is growing away from her. Meg is coming from hearing about a lovely wedding and confesses to being envious, which Jo says she is glad for so that Meg will never marry someone poor (as Mr. Brooke is). For the next two weeks, Jo acts very strangely, is rude to Mr. Brooke, attached to Meg, and always laughing with Laurie. Jo comes in one day with a newspaper story and reads it aloud to the girls, who quite like it, and are shocked to learn that Jo is the author. Jo is delighted that someday she may be able to write to support herself and help the family.

Analysis

This section of the book is very literary. Alcott employs Dickens's "Pickwick Society" to demonstrate a shared knowledge among her characters that brings them closer with one another and with any familiar readers. Laurie's exchange of "v" for "w" in "dewote" signifies all of the characters' familiarity with Dickens. Alcott includes a newspaper she produced as a child, and references her own works and poetry. As with *Pilgrim's Progress*, the girls' employment of a grand story of adventure to discuss their domestic dramas gives their experiences greater meaning and importance. The characters embrace this consciously when they climb up the hill to "Delectable Mountain" and look out over Boston, imagining it is their "Celestial

City."

Alcott includes and alludes to several of her own works, which enhance the realism of the book, a clearly intentional tactic, as Alcott stresses the *bona fide* nature of the newspaper. Her contemporary allusions also invite her readers to identify with the girls as similar to themselves, who have likely also cried over *Wide, Wide, World* or read about Flora McFlimsey in *Harper's Weekly*. The section concludes with Jo's first successful publications. However, there is a distinction drawn between the March family's and Laurie's references to characters and stories to enhance their conversation and Fred Vaughn's plagiarism from *The Sea Lion* while playing Rig-marole.

Work is another major theme in this section. The girls' experiment helps them find solace in balancing work and pleasure, even during their vacation. Kate Vaughn is surprised that Meg is a governess and is rude to the tutor Mr. Brooke. John defends work as a form of independence, and tells Meg "there is no place like America for us workers." Laurie finds work a cure for his irritability when he comes across the girls discussing their Castles in the Air. The castles they envision, though, are filled with genius and luxury, rather than housework.

The visit of the Vaughns provides one of the first opportunities for Alcott to portray the distinctly American traits of her characters, being "free and easy" rather than standoffish, fighting with the spirit of '76, and saying, "We don't cheat in America." As both Americans and Northerners, her characters embrace the term "Yankee" proudly. When Fred accuses Yanks of being tricky, Jo responds, "Yanks have a trick of being generous to their enemies." Kate Vaughn concludes that American girls are "demonstrative" but likeable.

In this section, several characters and the reader are informed of Mr. Brooke's affection for Meg, but Meg is still unaware. Thus, Alcott employs dramatic irony, whereby the reader interprets Mr. Brooke's and Jo's actions differently than Meg does. Jo is deeply upset about the changes she foresees, viewing Meg's marriage as a threat to the sanctity of the family. Becoming more womanly is Jo's particular burden, but the idea that womanhood threatens the family causes Jo to revert to childlike ways, running down the hill with Laurie.

Summary and Analysis of Chapter 15 through Chapter 19

Summary

Chapter 15 A Telegram

On a gray November day, just as Marmee arrives home, a telegram arrives from Washington Hospital informing Marmee that Father is very ill, and asking her to come at once. Mother, the girls, and Hannah feel the world changing. They gather in fear and hope, until Hannah recovers and finds work a cure for despair. All start running errands and making preparations. Mr. Laurence offers himself as an escort, but as he is too old, he insists that Mr. Brooke go instead. Meg is the first to learn of this, and is deeply grateful to him. Aunt March sends money with a chiding note.

Late that afternoon, Jo finally returns from town with a queer expression and $25, a significant sum of money. Everyone is shocked to learn she has sold her hair, in order to make Father comfortable and bring him home. She had to convince the barber to take it, helped by his wife, who had a son in the war. The family eats and prepares for bed, despite their concerns for Father.

Chapter 16 Letters

The early morning finds the girls diligently reading their guidebooks, seeking comfort in their time of worry. The girls agree to say goodbye to Marmee cheerfully, and not add to her woes. She leaves them in Hannah's care and Mr. Laurence's protection. She encourages them to stay busy with work and not to grieve or fear too heavily, Mr. Brooke takes Mrs. March to the train station in a carriage, and the girls turn to their work. When they see that Marmee had mended their stockings before leaving, they all cry together at her thoughtfulness. Hannah treats them with coffee, and then the girls go off to their days, Meg at the Kings, Jo to Aunt March, and Beth and Amy to help Hannah at home.

Mr. Brooke sends a telegraph as soon as they arrive in Washington, reporting that Mr. March is on the mend, and daily reports following. The girls are relieved that Father is mending, and all write of how Meg is acting as head of the house, Jo throwing herself haphazardly into work, Beth helping Hannah most with errands and chores, Amy staying sweet, Mr. Laurence sending over anything he can, and Laurie keeping everyone lively and as merry as possible.

Chapter 17 Little Faithful

After a week of their tremendous hard work and virtue, the girls become a little less faithful. Jo catches cold, Amy returns to her art, and Meg spends much time rereading Mr. Brooke's dispatches and writing to her Mother.

Beth keeps up with her chores and does many of her sisters' as well. She goes to see the Hummels every day, but when the baby gets sick, she asks Meg or Jo to go instead, to try to help. They all put it off until later, until Beth decides to go herself, despite feeling tired and achy. She returns home that evening, and Jo finds her in the medicine closet, reading about scarlet fever. The Hummel baby had died in her arms while the mother had gone to get the doctor, and when the doctor returned, he sent Beth home to take belladonna to prevent getting sick. Jo feels guilty and responsible for letting Beth go, rather than going herself. She wakes Hannah, who reassures everyone that Beth will be all right.

Jo and Meg had scarlet fever when they were babies, but Amy is sent to Aunt March's to prevent getting sick. She refuses to go, until Laurie promises to come visit her every day. Jo becomes Beth's nurse. Hannah says that, as Beth will be all right, they should not tell Mother and Father, who will just be anxious. They were instructed to mind Hannah, so the girls obey, despite disliking lying and being worried about Beth.

Chapter 18 Dark Days

In fact, Beth is quite sick, but Hannah tries to maintain a hopeful front. It is during Beth's illness that many come to appreciate the importance of her sweet, selfless role in their lives. Jo, nursing Beth, has her rough was softened by Beth's tenderness and virtue. The girls are surprised by how many friends shy Beth has, when the milkman and grocer ask after her. When Beth grows delirious, the girls beg to write to Mother, and Hannah says she will consider it, but the decision is made harder when a letter comes saying Mr. March has had a relapse and Mother is needed there.

On the first day of December, Dr. Bangs decides that it is time to send for Mrs. March. Jo sends the telegram and returns to find Laurie with a letter saying Mr. March is on the mend. She cries to Laurie, who comforts her and brings her a little medicinal wine. He then confesses that he had grown impatient with Hannah and had disobeyed her orders and sent for Mrs. March the day previously, and that she would arrive late that night. Jo, ecstatic, hugs Laurie, who timidly kisses Jo, who quickly remembers herself, blames the wine, and sends him off to rest. The news that Mother is coming sends a wave of fresh air through the house, and even Hannah is relieved. Beth, however, is still in the throng of the fever, unmoving and unwell. At two o'clock in the morning, Beth suddenly looks peaceful and free of pain, and Jo begins to mourn her loss. Hannah, waking, realizes that the fever has finally passed, and Beth is beginning to get well. Dr. Bangs confirms Hannah's belief, and they girls keep a long vigil until their mother arrives a few hours later.

Chapter 19 Amy's Will

While life at home during Beth's illness is trying for the girls, life for Amy with Aunt March is also difficult for her. Aunt March cares for Amy, but tries to raise her on discipline and demands, rather than the loving kindness to which Amy is accustomed. With Aunt March, Amy must do an extraordinary amount of housework, sewing, reading aloud, lessons, and has precious few moments of free time. Laurie keeps his promise to come every day to drive with her.

The maid Esther is very kind to her, showing her all of Aunt March's possessions and jewelry boxes. Amy wonders where everything will go when Aunt March dies, and Esther explains that Aunt March's will gives the jewelry to Amy and her sisters. Amy is to receive the turquoise ring, for Aunt March favors her. Learning this, Amy resolves to be good and earn the ring. Esther sets up Amy's dressing room as a space for prayer and meditation, which is a great comfort to Amy. In her quest to be good, Amy decides to write a will, with Esther's help, and asks Laurie to be a witness. Laurie mentions that Beth, feeling ill one day, had promised away her things as well. Amy, inspired by Beth's goodness, asks that all of her curls be cut off and locks distributed to her friends, making a great sacrifice.

Analysis

In this darker section of the book, the March family is threatened on several fronts. At first, when Marmee leaves, they turn to work, which Hannah considers Hannah considers a "panacea for most afflictions." Jo writes an ode to work and its ability to sweep out thoughts of sorrow from her mind. Yet after some time they relax. The experiment over vacation foreshadowed the girls' attempts to get on without Marmee; in that instance, Beth's bird was the victim, whereas in this case Beth herself falls ill.

Several of the sisters turn to their faith. The morning Marmee departs, all the girls read their guidebooks with greater attention and care. Marmee reminds them that whatever happens, they "can never be fatherless." Amy truly develops her faith in this section, in her chapel in Aunt March's house. Jo, who feels guilty for Beth's illness, questions her faith, feeling that she can't find God, and that the good and dear people die first. Laurie, though, comforts Jo, assuring her that God won't take Beth yet. Laurie's comfort helps bring Jo closer to God.

The experience also brings Mr. Brooke closer into the family. By naming him "Greatheart", the sisters include him in their *Pilgrim's Progress* play, a special cohort. The dramatic irony of the previous section is enhanced here -- now, the readers' knowledge of John's feelings for Meg allows us to understand the significance not only of his actions, but of hers as well. As Meg appreciates Mr. Brooke escorting her mother, rereading his dispatches from Washington, and dreaming of brown eyes, we realize she is falling in love with him before she does.

Jo also has a brief experience with romance when she flies at Laurie after he sends for her mother. She blames the wine for making her hysterical, reflecting Alcott's views on alcohol, and rejects Laurie's affections beyond friendship, as she will throughout the book.

By including letters, Alcott provides unique insight into their individual voices and styles. This is the longest excerpt of Hannah's dialect that the reader sees. The letters serve to deepen the characterization of the family members by illustrating their distinct cares and modes of expression. The inclusion of Hannah's, Laurie's, and Mr. Laurence's letters demonstrates the expansion of the March family to include dear friends, particularly in this time of crisis.

This section emphasizes the nobility of Beth's selflessness, which all learn from. Jo insists that Beth's illness is her fault, and devotes herself to nursing Beth back to health. In this, and in cutting her hair to send money to her Father, Jo appreciates the sweetness of making sacrifices to help the ones she loves. Meg learns to value the blessings of a happy home no money can buy, and Amy explicitly vows to imitate Beth and be less selfish, beginning with her will. The experience of Beth's sickness - particularly when Jo believes she has died, when indeed the fever has passed - foreshadows her eventual death.

Summary and Analysis of Chapter 20 through Chapter 23

Chapter 20 Confidential

Marmee's delayed arrival from the train is received with great tenderness and love. After delivering Mrs. March, Laurie rushes off to tell Amy and Aunt March the news. Amy patiently and selflessly suppresses her desire to see her mother and gains praise from Laurie and Aunt March, who gives Amy the turquoise ring for being so well-behaved.

However, Marmee does come to see Amy that afternoon, to her great delight. They sit together in Amy's little chapel and discuss Amy's quest to be good. Marmee is at first concerned by the ring, as she thinks Amy is too young, but Amy explains that she wants to wear the ring to remind herself not to be selfish, so that she will be loved as Beth is. Marmee applauds Amy's intention, and then returns to Beth.

That evening, Jo confides in Marmee that Mr. Brooke cares for Meg and has her glove. Marmee says Mr. Brooke grew quite close to her and Father at the hospital, and that John told them honestly about his care for Meg and his plan to earn a comfortable home before asking for her hand. Marmee and Father feel that John is a good man, though poor, but that Meg is too young to be engaged. Marmee asks Jo to keep the secret from Meg until Marmee can discern Meg's feelings for John. Jo believes John will romance Meg, and things will change, and their happy life will be spoilt. When Meg comes in, Marmee speaks of John fondly, and gauging Meg's response, decides that Meg "does not love John yet, but she will learn to."

Chapter 21 Laurie Makes Mischief, and Jo Makes Peace

Jo tries dearly to keep her Mother's secret, to the frustration of Meg and Laurie. Laurie, devising that the secret concerns Meg and John Brooke, plots to find out what it is. Meg receives a letter she thinks is from John, professing his love for her. Meg secretly responds that she is too young, and he must speak to her parents. John's response is surprise at Meg, disclaiming any knowledge of the first letter professing his love, and accusing Jo of playing tricks on Meg. Jo clears her name and realizes that Laurie wrote both of the notes and signed John's name. Jo runs to get Laurie, while Mrs. March tells Meg how Mr. Brooke truly feels. Meg is disenchanted with lovers at the moment, and wants only to be friends.

Mrs. March and Laurie have a private conversation, after which he apologizes sincerely to Meg and promises never to tell Mr. Brooke of the matter. Laurie looks so penitent that Jo forgives him, but does not show it, and later goes over to his house to make amends. She finds that Mr. Laurence and Laurie have fought, for Laurie refused to divulge his conversation with Mrs. March, so Mr. Laurence shook him. This infuriated Laurie, who felt that his grandfather should trust his word and not shake him like a child. Laurie refuses to go down to dinner until his grandfather apologizes, and speaks of running away with Jo to Washington to make him sorry. Jo is tempted, but realizes she has duties at home, and as a girl does not have the freedoms that Laurie does.

Jo goes to find Mr. Laurence convinces him to apologize to Laurie. She mentions that if Mr. Laurence is not careful, Laurie might impulsively run away. Jo regrets this comment immediately, seeing Mr. Laurence look at a picture of Laurie's father, who did run away. She then makes a joke of it, and makes peace again. Nevertheless, Meg now knows of John's feelings, thus mischief was made.

Chapter 22 Pleasant Meadows

As Christmas approaches, both Beth and Mr. March are recovering nicely, and Mr. March talks of coming home soon. All of the girls have been influenced for the better by Beth's illness, with Meg working cheerfully, Amy giving away her possessions, and Jo tenderly caring for her sister. On Christmas morning, Beth declares that she is so happy and that her life is complete except for Father's absence. The other sisters are also happy with their Christmas presents - Undine and Sintram for Jo; a copy of Madonna and Child for Amy; and a silk dress from Mr. Laurence for Meg.

Just at that moment, Laurie announces another Christmas present for the March family, and in walks Father. Even Beth finds the strength to run to Father and embrace him, her Christmas wish fulfilled. In the excitement, Mr. Brooke kisses Meg by mistake, and Mr. March mentions later how kind and supportive Mr. Brooke has been, to Jo's great annoyance. After dinner with the Laurences and Mr. Brooke, the March family, reunited, rests and celebrates together. They reflect on the year, a pleasant but difficult one, and Father remarks that the Pilgrims have come a long way, and their bundles will soon tumble off.

Father observes that Meg's hands, once pretty and smooth, are now burned and hardened but beautifully so, for Meg has replaced vanity with dedication to loving and industrious housekeeping. Jo has indeed become a little woman, still strong-willed, but not wild, and caring for Beth with maternal tenderness. Beth has overcome much of her bashfulness, and all are grateful to have her safe. Amy is patient, less vain, and as dedicated to shaping her character as her clay figurines.

The evening ends with Beth recalling part of *Pilgrim's Progress* where everyone comes to a beautiful meadow to rest. She sings an excerpt from the book, giving thanks for contentment and bliss.

Chapter 23 Aunt March Settles the Question

Despite the utter joy at having Father home, there is a lingering anxiety and uncertainty in the March house felt by the adults about Meg and John. Jo confronts

Meg, who says that if John asks her, she will kindly ask to remain friends, as she is too young.

Just at that moment, Mr. Brooke stops by to collect his umbrella and see Mr. March. Jo flees the room, leaving Meg to make her speech. Meg starts to leave as well, but John stops her, holding her hand, and asks if she cares about him at all, as he loves her so much. Meg, forgetting her speech, simply says she does not know. He asks her to try to learn, and Meg is quite flattered, but she sees a sense of satisfaction in his eyes, as if he expects her to say yes. Thinking of Annie Moffat, Meg suddenly starts acting coquettish as other girls do, saying she is not interested and being hurtful and distant. John is deeply hurt, and Meg feels guilty, but at that moment, Aunt March comes in.

Mr. Brooke steps into the study as Aunt March quizzes the blushing Meg. Aunt March tells Meg that if she accepts the poor Mr. Brooke, Aunt March will not give them a single penny. Aunt March's statement raises Meg's spirit of opposition, and Meg declares that she will marry whom she likes. She then defends John, expounding on his courage, goodness, and their willingness to wait and work hard. Aunt March storms out, and John rushes in, having heard all of Meg's remarks. He asks again if she might care for him, and once more passing up the chance to make her sensible speech, Meg agrees.

Jo returns and is shocked to find Meg sitting on John's knee, and even more so when John kisses her and calls her "Sister Jo." Jo runs to her parents and sends them downstairs, while she cries. Mr. Brooke eloquently argues his case, and convinces the Marches to allow the engagement, with hopes that in three years he will have a home, steady business, and can be married. Even Jo is moved by how happy Meg is, though she is devastated at losing her dear friend. She is comforted by Laurie and the sight of her family so happy.

Analysis

In this concluding section of Part I, the March sisters are rewarded for their year of self-improvement. The parallels between the beginning of the novel and the end are clear. The Christmas presents the girls receive mirror their wishes in the beginning of the book. Their true reward, though, is the praise and recognition of their Father, and their own happiness at having become better people. At the end, as in the beginning, we find the family enjoying each other, but now the family has grown to include the Laurences and Mr. Brooke.

The theme of poverty is discussed in the context of Mr. Brooke's suitability for Meg. Mr. and Mrs. March support the marriage despite John's poverty, as long as he can provide basic comforts. Meg, whose castle in the air included luxurious things and "heaps of money," decides to marry a poor but good man and sacrifice any support from Aunt March to do so. In this sense, Meg rejects the dictates of society and makes, in her mind, the moral choice.

Embracing morality does not always require rejecting society, as Jo demonstrates when she refuses to run away with Laurie. Jo accepts that because she is a girl, she is resigned to to "prunes and prisms", a colloquial term meaning proper words for ladies to use and a transformation from Jo's typical embrace of slang. Jo simultaneously objects to inequality of men and women while accepting that she is a "little woman."

Alcott continues to draw on *Pilgrim's Progress* to enhance the meaning of the girls' journeys. In the green meadows, Christian and his companion Hopeful enjoy a respite with delight and replenish their weary spirits, but they are not yet "at their journey's end." So too, Alcott turns her readers' attention to the future with Jo and Laurie discussing what might happen in three years. She then premises the disclosure of this knowledge on the readers' reception to the book, engaging them in dialogue with the text.

Summary and Analysis of Chapter 24 through Chapter 30

Chapter 24 Gossip

The narrator begins Part II with some "gossip" about the March family. Three years later, the war has ended, and Mr. March is a minister and still quietly heads the household as its conscience and guide. John Brooke served in the army, was wounded and discharged, and is working as a bookkeeper to earn a home for Meg. Meg is preparing for married life, learning housekeeping, and she is greatly in love, although occasionally envious of the grand wedding and life had by her newlywed friends Sallie and Ned Moffat. Dovecote, Meg's new home, is modest but fitted out with great care and love from family and friends. Even Aunt March, who swore not to give a penny, found a way to give a full set of linens through another relative.

Jo has devoted herself to writing and Beth, who was weakened permanently by the scarlet fever, and is forever struggling to get well. Amy works as a companion for Aunt March, who tempted Amy with drawing lessons. Laurie, at college to please his grandfather, spends a good deal of time frolicking and enjoying and helping friends, with the love of his grandfather and the Marches his best talisman against idle indulgence. Laurie often brings his college friends home, who enjoy Jo's boyish camaraderie and Amy's pretty and charming companionship. Laurie occasionally implies that he has feelings for Jo, but she spurns his overtures.

Chapter 25 The First Wedding

Meg's wedding is simple, as she wants everything plain, honest, and surrounded with love. She made her own wedding dress, with only flowers for accessories. Aunt March is scandalized when she arrives and is welcomed by the bride herself. During the ceremony, the vows are said with great earnestness and love, Meg gives the first kiss for Marmee and her sisters.

In the three years passed, Jo's face and tongue have softened and her hair has grown long. Beth is pale and thin, still weak, but cheerful. Amy has truly blossomed, now sixteen, and full of poise. The luncheon is simple, with the wine sent by Mr. Laurence and Aunt March nowhere to be found, of which Mr. and Mrs. March disapprove. Meg tells Laurie this, and upon learning that he occasionally drinks, she uses the occasion to ask Laurie to avoid drinking in the future by making a temperance pledge, which he does.

After the wedding, all exclaim what a beauty it was, despite the simplicity. Mr. Laurence tells Laurie that if he ever wants to marry, he hopes Laurie will choose a March girl, and Laurie says he will do his best. Meg's married life begins.

Chapter 26 Artistic Attempts

Pursuing her ambition to become a great artist, Amy has tried various forms of art to the entertainment of her family, from poker sketching to painting to charcoal to sculpting, which ends in when an attempt to make a plaster mold of her foot goes awry. Meanwhile, she also strives to be an accomplished lady, which is easier for her, being naturally tactful and pleasing.

In an effort to be aristocratic, Amy plans a small party for her classmates in drawing school and insists on offering the comforts to which her rich friends are accustomed, including an expensive lunch. Marmee tries to advise her to stay in keeping with their circumstances, but Amy refuses, saying she will pay for it herself, and Marmee allows experience to be the teacher. Unfortunately, the party does not go as planned. The first attempt is postponed to the next day due to rain after all the preparations have been made. The following Amy has to go buy a lobster, and is embarrassed when she runs into one of Laurie's college friends. After preparing for the party, she is dismayed when only one girl comes. Amy is an excellent host, and the girl is very kind, but after she leaves the family has a good laugh about Amy's misadventure.

Chapter 27 Literary Lessons

Jo, wishing to be a writer, spends great time in the garret when she feels inspired, often foregoing meals and sleep to translate her imagination into stories. One day, while accompanying Miss Crocker to a lecture, she learns that sensational stories like those by Mrs. S.L.A.N.G. Northbury have quite an audience, and a newspaper is having a competition for such stories with a prize of $100. Jo secretly writes a story about an earthquake in Lisbon and submits it to the competition. Six long weeks later, Jo receives a note of encouragement and the grand prize, for $100. Her family celebrates, though her unworldly Father says that she can do better, and should aim higher, disregarding the money. Jo, however, continues to write, and takes great pride in assisting with the family's bills. Her $100 sends Beth and Marmee to the shore for relaxation and recovery, and several more stories pay for the butcher bill, groceries, and new carpet. Jo cherishes her independence and ability to help her family.

Encouraged by her success, Jo writes her first novel. After much effort, she finds a publisher, but he insists that she remove 1/3 of the story. In her redrafting, she tries to please everyone, and thus pleases no one, least of all herself. It is published, and she receives $300 and heaps of criticism and praise, furthering her confusion, but she is glad for the trial.

Chapter 28 Domestic Experiences

Meg and John have a wonderful but trying time adjusting to married life. Their first big fight comes about after Meg tries to make currant jelly. After a day of boiling, sugaring, and straining their entire crop of currants, Meg is unable to make the jelly, and ends the day crying with exhaustion. Unfortunately, on this day John brought home a colleague for dinner, as Meg had often encouraged him to do. Finding the house in disarray, dinner uncooked, and Meg tired and cranky, John has to play host with an impromptu dinner. Both Meg and John feel betrayed and hurt, and neither wants to apologize first, until Meg gives in. John also apologizes and their first real disagreement is smoothed over.

Meg also struggles with envying the luxurious items Sallie Moffat has. On her shopping ships with Sallie, she begins to buy a trifle here, and a trifle there, and then spends fifty dollars on silk for a new dress. Meg feels deeply guilty, even more so tells John. He is angry, and Meg tries to justify herself, saying she is tired of being poor. Meg immediately regrets her comment, and though John quickly forgives her, she feels awful. John works later hours and cancels an order of a coat for himself to cover his expenses. Meg and John have a long, open conversation about their poverty and the strength of character it gives them. The next day Meg swallows her pride and asks Sallie to buy the silk from her, then uses the money to buy John's coat, and never again wastes his money.

Several months later, Meg gives birth to twins, Daisy and Demi, which are nicknames for Margaret and John.

Chapter 29 Calls

Amy and Jo prepare to make formal calls to families around town, to Jo's great consternation. Amy dresses Jo and instructs her in how to carry herself and behave at each house so she will be liked, but Jo, annoyed by the exercise of trying to win others' approval, acts inappropriately at every home. Jo imitates one of Amy's friends May Chester, and then she is rude to a titled gentleman. At their final call on Aunt March, they also find her engrossed in conversation with Aunt Carrol. They discuss a fair that the Chesters are having to support the freedmen, at which Amy has been offered a chance to volunteer, and of which Jo disapproves. Aunt Carrol and Aunt March appreciate Amy's gratitude toward the Chesters, and Jo pronounces that she does not like favors. Aunt March and Aunt Carrol look at each other knowingly then ask the girls if they speak French. Amy does, a little, but Jo refuses to learn. Jo proposes they leave promptly, and the two Aunts seem quite decided about something.

Chapter 30 Consequences

After spending long hours preparing to work the art table at the Chesters' fair, making her own pieces and soliciting ones from others, Amy is asked by Mrs. Chester to move to the flower table. May Chester is jealous of Amy, whose art was prettier, who was danced with more often. May also heard rumors that Amy mocked her recently, though in fact this was Jo. Amy understands the slight, but accepts politely, removes her artwork from the table, and spends the entire evening setting up the previously neglected flowers.

At home, Amy explains that she does not wish to be mean simply because the Chesters were, and her mother agrees that kindness is often our best weapon against our enemies. The next morning, while reading a book of sayings she illustrated, she is reminded to “love thy neighbor” and inspired to return her artwork to the art table where May now works. Amy is proud of being generous in the face of meanness, despite the long day spent alone at the flower table, looking wistfully at the busy and popular art table.

At home, Jo conspires to get her revenge. She asks Laurie to send over some fresh, new flowers, and to have his troupe of friends shower Amy’s table with attention. Laurie agrees wholeheartedly, though giving Jo such plaintive and suggestive looks that she shuts the door in his face. The troupe indeed makes Amy’s table a great success. Jo learns that May has seen her error and made sure all of Amy’s works sold, so Amy sends the troupe to May’s table to do their duty. Jo admires Amy’s generous spirit and gives her great respect, and Amy explains that, for her, being a lady means being truly well mannered, in behavior as well as speech. Jo trusts that Amy will be rewarded in time for her efforts.

Amy gets her reward just one week later, in the form of an invitation to accompany Aunt Carrol to Europe. Jo is shocked and hurt that Amy has been invited rather than Jo, feeling that Amy is too young. However, Aunt Carrol writes of Jo’s disinclination toward favors and French that Jo had thoughtlessly shared during their call. Marmee urges Jo not to spoil Amy’s happiness, and Beth is grateful that Jo will stay at home near her. Jo tries, and is helpful and happy getting Amy ready to go, at which point she sobs with regret and frustration. Amy is also cheerful until she leaves her family, and begs Laurie to watch over them. He promises to do so, and to come comfort her if anything should happen, not realizing he would truly need to.

Analysis

Alcott begins Part II by addressing her readers, continuing her ongoing conversation with them. She knows her young readers will not object to the "lovering" for she has received countless letters from them demanding exactly that. She is also clear in foreshadowing the events to come, giving the readers' greater insight than her characters have, particularly when Jo and Amy are calling on Aunt March and Aunt Carrol. The interactions between Laurie and Jo also hint at developments to come.

Flowers, particularly roses, are a recurrent motif in Part II of Little Women. At Meg's wedding, Alcott personifies the roses. Meg's choice of wearing John's favorite roses rather than fashionable orange flowers symbolizes her wish for a genuine and simple marriage. This shows Meg's growth since she went to "Vanity Fair." At the Chesters' fair, Amy is relegated to the flower table, but through the help of her friends and family, she beautifies it nicely.

Family is still the primary concern for the characters in the book, although their attentions begin to turn outward. Meg's concern is also familial, although she is focused on making a happy family of her own, and she and John work through their concerns independently, utilizing the advice but not interference of the Marches. This outward shift in focus is reflected in the difference in the allusions Alcott makes, compared to Part I. Alcott abandons the *Pilgrim's Progress* allegory, which her characters have outgrown. Laurie alludes to "Jupiter Ammon," signifying his advanced education, Amy is compared to foreign artists, and Marmee to Maria Theresa, a Roman-German empress. Jo often alludes to Shakespeare as well as Keats and Tennyson, noting her more literary focus.

The characters are still concerned with morality, though not necessarily in the views of society. Laurie feels the conflict between what is socially easy and what is moral when Meg asks him to take the temperance pledge. His choice falls within the March's moral code and within Alcott's, as she advocated temperance. Jo devises her own moral guide to her calls with Amy, wishing to be polite to those she likes and rude to those she does not, regardless of what is proper.

Amy's attempted dinner party is also an example of the failure of her efforts to please society. When Jo agrees to help, Alcott alludes to Mrs. Grundy, a character in a Thomas Morton play who represents propriety and society's good opinion. Despite Marmee's advice, Amy tries to meet society's expectations, rather than those suited to her poverty, with laughable results. When Amy is being pleasing to society by being kind and gracious, however, she is highly rewarded. Her polite calls and generous behavior at the Chesters' fair are rewarded with a trip abroad.

Jo's discovery of the audience for sensation stories written by Mrs. S.L.A.N.G. Northbury is a parody of the writer Mrs. E.D.E.N. Southworth, who published stories in the mid-nineteenth century. By drawing on her own experiences and alluding to contemporary authors, Alcott continues to make her story realistic and timely.

Jo's first try at a sensation story does not contradict her moral code, as the earthquake in Lisbon in 1755 was considered punishment for the sinners of that city. In trying to please society with her book, however, Jo gets the worst of it. Alcott alludes to Aesop's fable of the donkey and the old man, where the old man, trying to please everyone, ends up drowning the donkey. This experience was based directly on Alcott's experience -- not with Part I, which was largely published as written, but rather with *Moods*, published in 1864.

Summary and Analysis of Chapter 31 through Chapter 36

Summary

Chapter 31 Our Foreign Correspondent

We learn of Amy's travels through her letters home. She describes the ship to Ireland and the train to London in picturesque detail, her artistic eye soaking up the colors and scenery. She enjoys traveling very much, including the attentions of several gentlemen along the way. London is rainy, but Amy enjoys shopping with her aunt. She is surprised to find Fred and Frank Vaughn come calling at tea, and enjoys laughing about Camp Laurence and going to the theater with them.

The Vaughns are great hosts in London, taking Amy and her cousin Florence to museums and picnics. They are sad to part ways when the Carrols and Amy go to France, but they hope to meet in Rome. Amy particularly enjoys Fred, who then surprises them by turning up in Paris. They are thankful to have him along for company and translation. Amy is delighted by the Louvre, and is enjoying Fred's company more and more.

Next, they sail up the Rhine, and Fred befriends some students who help him serenade Amy and Flo by moonlight. In Germany, Amy wishes she had read more, particularly Goethe. Fred gambles some money, and Amy says she thinks he needs someone to marry and look after him. Amy realizes that Fred has affections for her, and in her eminently practical way, decides that she will accept him if he asks. Fred is very rich, relatively enjoyable, and she thinks they could learn to be fond of each other. Amy wishes more to live in comfort than to be in love. Fred learns that Frank is ill and rushes away, but asks Amy not to forget him, and they plan to meet in Rome.

Chapter 32 Tender Troubles

Marmee notices that something is troubling Beth, for she has been quite sad, and asks Jo to find out Beth's secret. After observing her, Jo decides that Beth is in love with Laurie. Jo insists to herself that she will make Laurie love Beth back. In fact, Laurie has been trying to express his affections toward Jo, but she ignores or denies him. Jo hopes Laurie might learn to love Beth, particularly if Jo went away.

While pondering what to do, Jo finds herself in a conversation with Laurie about flirting, which he does quite a bit, but does not admire in excess in others, and at which Jo is hopeless. Jo advises Laurie to devote himself to a modest girl – meaning Beth – once he is through with college and deserving of her. Laurie, thinking Jo means herself, is encouraged and humbled. He starts behaving more seriously and speaking of "turning a new leaf."

That evening, Jo finds Beth crying herself to sleep over a new pain. She will not tell Jo what it is, for Jo can do nothing to help, but promises to tell her in time. Jo, believing Beth's heart is aching over Laurie, comforts her. The next day, Jo decides to spend the winter working as a teacher in a boardinghouse in New York for the daughters of Mrs. Kirke, one of Marmee's friends. Jo tells Marmee that she feels Laurie is getting too fond of her, and she does not return the feelings. Marmee is thankful for Jo's feelings, as she feels the two would be too strong-willed a match. Jo divulges that she thinks Beth might like Laurie, which Marmee does not believe, but still feels Jo should go away for Laurie's sake.

Jo asks Beth to look after Laurie for her. Laurie simply tells Jo that going away will not do any good.

Chapter 33 Jo's Journal

Jo's letters describe her new home, a funny room in the boardinghouse, and her two pupils. Mrs. Kirke is quite kind, but busy, and Jo finds herself bashful in the big house. Jo observes Professor Bhaer, an older, poor German who tutors to support his nephews. As her pupils' nursery is next to Mr. Bhaer's study, she often listens to him humming Goethe or observes him teaching and playing with the children, doing kind things for the servants, and discussing philosophy with the young men. Jo also befriends Miss Norton, a rich gentlewoman at the house. Jo and the Professor become good friends, since they both have lively spirits and enjoy children and literature. Out of thanks for his kindness, Jo asks Mrs. Kirke if she might help with mending Mr. Bhaer's clothes, which he does himself, and in return, Mr. Bhaer gives her German lessons. At New Year's they exchange gifts, and their friendship flourishes beautifully. Jo is grateful for her friend, as she does not enjoy the "whippersnappers" in the house. At a masquerade ball, she goes down and is quite sociable and theatrical, and all are surprised at the unmasking that it was Jo all along.

Chapter 34 A Friend

For many years, Jo has wished to be wealthy, so that she could give make Beth comfortable, go abroad, and always have more than enough so she could share it with others. So, following her success with her prize money writing sensation stories, she continues to do so in New York for a paper called the Weekly Volcano. The editor accepts her first story only when all moral elements have been cut out, which alarms Jo, but for $25 a story she obliges. To keep her plots fresh and her stories thrilling, Jo finds herself including increasingly lurid material, which she seeks out in newspaper articles and ancient tales. She publishes anonymously and does not share the news at home, feeling they would not approve. Jo therefore stays focused on the ends, rather than the means, of her earnings.

In her new study of characters, real and imaginary, Jo finds that Mr. Bhaer is a real live hero. Wondering why he is so well loved, not being rich, handsome, or young, she decides it is his benevolence, his simple joyful attitude and goodwill towards his fellow men and women. She learned that in Germany he had been an honored Professor, though here he was a humble tutor, and never mentions his true intellect and position. When Jo attends a literary symposium with the kind Miss Norton, she is quite disillusioned by seeing authors, scientists, and musicians whose work she admires are still in society and flirt and eat and gossip just as much as anyone. Jo finds herself fascinated by a conversation about philosophy that seems to undermine religion and place intellectualism in its place. Mr. Bhaer, concerned about her and other young people being drawn into this tempting but empty system of thought, speaks out in defense of religion and morality. Jo, feeling the world is righted again, deepens her respect and admiration for him.

During one of their German lessons, Mr. Bhaer sees a newspaper story like the one that Jo secretly writes. He shares his disgust that such rubbish comes into the house, and his disapproval of those who write it. Jo blushes, and says the stories may only be silly, and their authors good. Mr. Bhaer realizes she may be writing such material and, remembering that she is far from the moral compass of home, says not all demands should be met, and the living made from meeting such immoral demands is not honest. After they part, Jo rereads her stories and decides she agrees with Mr. Bhaer, and burns them up. She tries writing moral stories and children's stories, but does not find a demand, and stops writing for the rest of her time in New York. Instead, she deepens her friendship with Mr. Bhaer and all are very sad when she is to leave in June. At their parting, Jo invites him to visit, but then mistakenly blushes when she speaks of Laurie, and Mr. Bhaer gets the impression that she loves Laurie. That evening, alone in his room, he laments that to be with Jo is not for him.

Chapter 35 Heartache

Laurie, who worked ardently while Jo was away, grew his hair as she likes, and gave up billiards, graduates from college with honors and makes everyone proud. The day he returns from college, Jo meets him, fearing he may propose. Jo is right, as Laurie admits that he has loved her since the moment he met her, and tells how hard he has worked to earn her favor. Jo apologizes, saying she has tried to love him but does not, and cannot lie. Laurie accuses her of loving Mr. Bhaer, which almost makes Jo laugh, since it is so far from her mind. She tries to reason with him, but Laurie is deeply hurt, and tries to convince Jo that everyone expects it, and that they should not disappoint. However, Jo agrees with Marmee that they are too quick-tempered and strong-willed, and cannot marry. Jo says he should marry someone more fashionable and accomplished, and angry Laurie storms off saying he is going "to the devil." This alarms Jo, who goes straight to Mr. Laurence and tells him what happened. Mr. Laurence, disappointed but kind, shares Jo's fears about Laurie's impetuousness and devises a plan for him to travel with Laurie abroad. Mr. Laurence will take care of business in London and visit friends in Paris, while Laurie can travel as he likes. When introducing the plan to Laurie that evening, Mr. Laurence artfully mentions music and adventures, and Laurie agrees to go. In but a few weeks they are gone. Jo feels that she has stabbed her best friend in the heart, and her boy Laurie will return a changed man.

Chapter 36 Beth's Secret

When Jo returns from New York, she notices a change in Beth, as if the mortal is fading away and the immortal is starting to shine through. She proposes a trip to the mountains with her newspaper earnings, but Beth begs to stay closer to home, so she and Jo go to the seashore for a few weeks. It is here that Jo realizes that Beth's secret all along was not that she loves Laurie, but that Beth is dying. Beth says she does hope Laurie will be her brother someday, and Jo says Amy has left for him. Beth explains that she was sad in the fall because she had given up hope on living. She did not want to speak of it, not being sure, but she has since made her peace with it, and bravely, and piously now simply waits and tries to be willing. Jo still hopes something might change, but Beth says she has faith, and a feeling that she was not intended to live long, not having made the great plans and ambitions the others had. She does not share Jo's hope of getting well, but wishes to enjoy peacefully their remaining time together, and asks Jo to help Mother and Father bear it. Jo agrees, and dedicates herself heart and soul to her sister.

When they return, Mother and Father see the change in Beth, and understand the truth without words.

Analysis

The letters from both Jo and Amy encourage us to compare and contrast their experiences, as Jo points out often. Alcott encourages this comparison by having the girls refer to one another and make similar allusions, such as to Goethe. Both girls, away from home, are compromising their morality for money. Both are befriending potential suitors, though the suitors themselves are quite different. Fred is not honorable, but he is rich, while Professor Bhaer is the opposite. The comparison allows the reader to understand the similar challenges a young woman at this time faces while allowing for different contexts and decisions by the women.

Jo's struggle with morality is largely contained in her writing. Jo is driven to compromise her morals for money, much as Amy is. At the literary symposium, Jo is struck by the human fallibility of many revered authors. Her allusions are largely to eighteenth and nineteenth century authors, in part implicating them and their works. Alcott had attended many such symposia, and it is likely that Jo's disillusionment is drawn from Alcott's own experiences.

In praising Mr. Bhaer by using the words of a "wise man," Alcott quotes Ralph Waldo Emerson. Alcott befriended Emerson as well as several other New England thinkers and author through her father's philosophical circle. The Speculative Philosophers reference thinkers admired by the Transcendentalist philosophers like Alcott's father, but it is clear that Jo prefers Mr. Bhaer's philosophy.

Alcott conveys Mr. Bhaer's broken English dialect much as she does Hannah's. Jo and Mr. Bhaer's sharing German recalls John translating and reading German with

Meg. The song Jo first hears Mr. Bhaer humming is the same song she will ask him to sing much later, when he visits her house, and looks at her plaintively, imbuing the song with new meaning.

When Jo returns from New York, her focus is on Beth. Jo is the first to foreshadow Laurie marrying Amy, which helps convince the reader that it is the right choice, a difficult argument for Alcott. Unfortunately, Jo mistakenly gives Laurie hope, encouraging him to work hard and earn the affections of a modest girl - meaning Beth, though Jo thinks she means herself. This case of dramatic irony brings the reader in on Alcott's secret and helps prepare them. Jo and Marmee's conversation about Laurie also gives the reader insight into why Jo should not marry Laurie, and foreshadows Jo's response to Laurie's proposal.

Summary and Analysis of Chapter 37 through Chapter 41

Summary

Chapter 37 New Impressions

At Christmas, Laurie comes to Nice to see Amy. They are delighted to have reminders of home. Amy feels often that she ought to go home to see Beth, but her family says stay. Laurie and Amy gather new impressions of each other after a year apart. Both feel the other have grown from children into young adults. Amy, who does not know about Laurie's proposal and Jo's rejection, finds Laurie a bit indifferent and almost blasé. Laurie finds Amy an elegant and graceful young woman, but maintaining her native spirit.

Amy invites Laurie to a Christmas ball that evening, and arranges herself quite nicely to make a good impression on the gentleman. Laurie does admire and compliment her, but she encourages him to be blunt and natural, like they were at home. Laurie's casual attitude toward her frustrates Amy, who is in high demand by other gentlemen. Watching her dance, lively and properly, Laurie grows in admiration, and is much more attentive when she returns. He is impressed that she has made so much of her opportunity to live and travel overseas. He signs up for all of the remaining dances, and the two enjoy a lovely evening together.

Chapter 38 On the Shelf

With Daisy and Demi, Meg and John's twins, come new challenges for the couple. Meg is completely absorbed in her babies for the first year of their lives, to the detriment of her happiness, John's, and their relationship. Meg ceases to give John her attention and time, and John responds by spending more time out of the house with friends. Once Daisy and Demi start to calm down and need less of her constant care, Meg finds herself alone at home in the evenings and misses John's company. She does not want to ask him to stay home, and so they continue, missing one another, until Marmee learns of the situation. Marmee shows Meg that in her duty to her children, she has forgotten her duty to her husband. She encourages Meg to include John in raising the children, especially Demi, drawing on her own experience with Mr. March. She encourages Meg to do more housework while Hannah attends to the babies and to take interest in the world's affairs, since they affect her as well as any man. Meg agrees, and surprises John with a nice supper and an attentive wife. Demi tries to join the supper, and learns that John is much stricter on discipline than Meg. This is initially hard for Meg, but she learns to trust that John will be kind as well as firm. They each try to take interest in the other's concerns of politics and sewing, and agree to go out more and make home more enjoyable for all, to great success.

Chapter 39 Lazy Laurence

Laurie stays a month in Nice, rather than a week as he planned, as both he and Amy enjoy each other's companionship. One day they go to Valrosa and Amy sketches him and decides to find out what has changed. She and worries that he has gotten into trouble gambling or loving a married woman, but Laurie assures her that he has stayed out of mischief. He asks when she will become a great artist, but Amy divulges that Rome humbled her, made her see that her talent was not genius, and so she intends to be an ornament to society. Laurie admires her new goal, and suggests that Fred Vaughn might give her an opportunity. Amy is reserved in her reply, but admits that she will marry Fred if he asks, despite not feeling strong affection for her. Laurie is surprised and disappointed, saying that Fred is not the type he would have thought Amy to like.

Amy then lectures Laurie on his indolence of late, and urges him to go to his grandfather as he says he will, and be useful. Amy tells him she despises him for his lazy selfishness, which squanders his opportunities of money, health, and good position. Amy wishes Jo were there to help her, and seeing Laurie's reaction, realizes what they never told her at home, that Jo refused him. Laurie confirms her realization, and Amy apologizes for being unkind, though encourages him to accept defeat more resolutely, and do something to make Jo love him, or be respected, if he cannot be loved. By graduating well, Laurie showed that he could accomplish great tasks if he tries, but he just needs another motivation now. Amy concludes her lecture by showing him her sketch of him and comparing it to an earlier, rougher sketch of him years ago taming a horse—active, energetic, and full of life. The next day Amy receives a note that Laurie has gone to his grandfather, like a good boy.

Chapter 40 The Valley of the Shadow

At home, everyone does her best to make Beth's remaining time happy. A room is set up for her with her piano and worktable and everyone's nicest trinkets and pleasures. Beth, never idle, sits and makes gifts to drop out the window to the schoolchildren passing below. This sunny time together, with the family spending time reading and working in one room, prepares them for the hard time to come, when Beth feels pain and exhaustion. Jo sleeps on a couch in the room to be always near, feeling that nursing sweet Beth is the highest honor of her life to date. This time teaches Jo patience, duty, tenderness, and faith, and she recognizes the beauty of her sister's simple and humble life. She composes a poem of admiration to Beth's life and gratitude for all Beth taught her, which Beth finds to her great comfort, as her one regret was the fear that she had wasted her life and been useless. Jo says Beth will continue to be with her, in all that she has learned, and Beth asks Jo to take her place at home and be strong for Mother and Father. Jo agrees, taking up this new goal and giving up her dreams of being a great writer or traveling abroad.

Beth dies quietly and peacefully that spring, and those who loved her most are thankful that she is finally at rest.

Chapter 41 Learning to Forget

Amy's lecture did make Laurie realize that he had been lazy and selfish. He goes to Vienna to try to earn Jo's respect, if not her love, by writing a Requiem or an opera. He finds, though, that tomboy Jo makes a difficult heroine, and instead uses memories of Amy as his model. Yet after attending an opera by Mozart, Laurie agrees with Amy that talent is not genius, becomes humble, and accepts that he will not be a great musician. Having given up his dream, he wonders what to do next. During this time, he finds himself forgetting his romantic love of Jo, feeling only a brotherly warmth toward her, despite all his sincerest intentions to love her all his life. He writes her to ask, one last time, if she will have him, and her response confirms that she never will. She urges Laurie to attend to Amy, for whom it is difficult to be far from home with Beth so sick. After finally saying goodbye to his love for Jo, Laurie begins a correspondence with Amy, who is indeed homesick, and they write to one another often. Laurie leaves Vienna and goes to Paris, hoping that Amy will ask him to visit Nice.

Amy wishes to see Laurie, but does not invite him, for Fred Vaughn has returned. Troubled by Laurie's view of her potential engagement, and her own misgivings, Amy found herself declining Fred's offer, to her own surprise. She enjoys writing to Laurie very much, both of them cherishing each other's letters in ways they feel are brotherly and sisterly, but are truly romantic. Laurie is relieved to know that Fred has gone to Egypt, understanding that Amy turned him down.

Amy is in Vevey with the Carrols when she learns that Beth has died. Laurie goes to her right away, and finds her sitting in a garden, a rare chance to see Amy's tender side. Amy runs to Laurie when she sees him, and as they embrace, both feel the truth, that they love each other, but they do not speak of it. They are great comforts to each other in this sorrowful time, and Aunt Carrol discretely encourages the match. Laurie and Amy are very active in Vevey, and Amy admires the change wrought in him. Laurie feels guilty at first for replacing Jo with Amy, but he feels his new love is genuine, and waits for the time to say something. That time comes when they are rowing together on a lake, very simply and beautifully, and Amy accepts.

Analysis

The theme of work is discussed in this section in Amy's lecture of Laurie. She despises him because he is lazy and wasteful with money. Laurie always struggled with indolence; indeed, laziness, and wanting to pursue music rather than work for his grandfather, and loving Jo are Laurie's three main burdens. At Amy's urging, Laurie overcomes all three challenges in this section. Amy also overcomes her selfishness in denying Fred Vaughn.

In contrast to Laurie is industrious Beth. Beth's death draws out several key themes of the book. Her own selflessness is celebrated and revered. Her self-improvement continues to the end, striving to accept death cheerfully and faithfully. Beth asks Jo to care dutifully for Mother and Father, and Jo agrees, sacrificing her own dreams and ambitions. She makes this sacrifice in part after learning the beauty of selflessness from Beth herself.

Beth's death is also the impetus to bring Laurie and Amy together. Their joining is romantic, but is also an act of making the family whole. Throughout the book, several characters refer to wanting Laurie to be officially part of their family.

The motif of flowers continues to prevalent in this section. At the Christmas Ball in Nice, Amy's use of flowers as her ornamentation makes Laurie admire her for covering "poverty with flowers." At Valrosa, Laurie pricks himself on a thorny rose and thinks of Jo, and Amy gives him smaller, cream-colored ones, butting them in his buttonhole as she has seen lovers do. Laurie at first thinks the cream roses symbolize death, which foreshadows the loss of Beth, but later associates them with Amy. In this exchange, Alcott foreshadows his proposal, choosing Amy instead of Jo. Amy continues to send Laurie pressed roses in her letters.

In Meg and John's struggles with domesticity, the themes of duty and women's rights are relevant. Meg feels John is not fulfilling his duty to her, when in fact she is the culprit. Marmee urges her to balance her duty to children and to husband. This domestic focus appears to subjugate women to the household, even if they are the rulers there, but Marmee also encourages Meg to stay interested in the world beyond the house. While Meg is not particularly able to follow politics, Marmee knows that they do affect her, as evidenced by the Civil War that took Father away.

Summary and Analysis of Chapter 42 through Chapter 47

Summary

Chapter 42 All Alone

Despite her preparation, Jo is devastated at losing Beth, and feels despair at spending life attending only to household worries. She is comforted by her Mother, who shares her sorrow, and by her Father, whose ministry and counsel she seeks out. Through her work she tries to adopt Beth's spirit of cheerful housekeeping, taking care to make home cozy and comfortable. Jo sees how improved Meg is through her marriage, particularly her children, and wonders if it might in fact be enjoyable for her.

In the meantime, Mother suggests writing as a way for Jo to find more joy. Jo is wary, but finds herself writing a simple story that is greatly received by family, then friends, and even newspapers. Jo wonders at her success, but Father explains that rather than writing for money, Jo is simply writing the truth, with a direct simplicity that speaks to people's hearts.

When Laurie and Amy write of their engagement, Jo is genuinely happy for them, but begins to wish to find the love and joy they have. She wanders to the garret, where she comes across reminders of her winter in New York and Mr. Bhaer's friendship, and wishes to see him again.

Chapter 43 Surprises

The day before her twenty-fifth birthday, Jo laments that she will be a literary spinster. The narrator here urges readers to be kind and respectful to spinsters, as there is tragedy and sacrifice often in their histories, and remember the kindnesses that countless Aunts have shown them. Jo is surprised out of her reverie by Laurie, who has returned from abroad with Amy. They are awkward for a moment, but they are delighted to see each other and rekindle their exuberant friendship, and Laurie lets slip that he and Amy had gotten married, so that she could accompany him and Grandfather back home while the Carrols stayed another year abroad. Laurie explains to Jo that he does still love her, as a brother, and that it would have all come about naturally if he had been sensible and not proposed, as Jo urged. He asks if they can go back to being best friends as they were, and Jo assures him that they can be friends, but now as man and woman, and not as children as they were before. Having Laurie nearby is a great cheer to Jo, and when the entire family troops in, joy is plentiful all around, with gentle sad reminders of dear Beth, as when Mr. Laurence asks Jo to be his girl now.

After tea, the party goes upstairs, leaving Jo to feel lonely again just for a moment, when there is a knock at the door, and she finds Mr. Bhaer has come to visit. She invites him in and proudly introduces him to the family, where is he is a quick favorite. Mr. Bhaer and Father are kindred spirits, the babies enjoy his pockets of treats, and even Laurie overcomes his brotherly suspicion of the man's intentions. Mr. Bhaer looks wistfully and Laurie and occasionally at Jo, until he learns that Laurie has married Amy, to his delight. The evening ends with Amy leading them through Beth's old songs, and Mr. Bhaer and Jo singing a duet. Mr. Bhaer promises to come again, for he has business in town, and all pronounce their approval of him.

Chapter 44 My Lord and Lady

Laurie and Amy discuss the potential of Mr. Bhaer marrying Jo, and wish they could help his poverty without hurting their pride. Laurie reassures Amy that he will be fully glad for Jo, without remorse, and Amy reassures Laurie that she would have married him if he were a pauper. They lament that there are girls who do marry for money, and gentleman and ladies who are ambitious but poor, to proud to ask for help. They commit to sharing their blessings with others less fortunate, particularly young women with artistic talents, and feel their love strengthened by their wish to share it.

Chapter 45 Daisy and Demi

The narrator insists on describing Daisy and Demi. Both are quite precocious, with Daisy modeling housekeeping and Demi energetically modeling machine making. Daisy is a sweet creature, whose angelic nature reminds the family of Beth, though she is not shy. Demi loves to understand how things work, including his own body and mind, and reasons with his Mother about their rules. Both love Jo, or "Aunt Dodo," and are saddened when Mr. Bhaer's visits take her time and attention away from them, though they enjoy his company and chocolates. Seeing Mr. Bhaer give Jo a chocolate, Demi asks him if great boys like great girls, to the embarrassment of all. It is then that Mr. March realizes that Mr. Bhaer has not been visiting entirely to speak with him about philosophy, but also to woo Jo, though neither Jo nor Mr. Bhaer have spoken of it.

Chapter 46 Under the Umbrella

During Mr. Bhaer's frequent visits from town, all realize the love that is growing between him and Jo, and see Jo's spirits rise, though no one says a word. Jo, though, is afraid that after years of denouncing love, Laurie especially will tease and laugh.

After a fortnight of such visits, Mr. Bhaer stays away for a few days. Feeling cross, Jo goes into town on the pretense of doing errands, though she walks by the shops instead, hoping to see him. When it begins to rain, Jo chides herself, until she finds an umbrella above her, and Mr. Bhaer holding it. He asks if he may walk with her, and she agrees happily. In an effort to stay calm, Jo gives Mr. Bhaer the mistaken impression she does not have feelings for him, and he tells her that he has found a place teaching at a college in the West, and he will leave tomorrow. Jo hides her disappointment while Mr. Bhaer stops to buy treats for his last visit to the Marches.

After shopping, Mr. Bhaer proposes to go to the house, for which Jo is grateful. The rain and long day, and the prospect of Mr. Bhaer's leaving make her quite sad, and she quietly begins to cry. Mr. Bhaer asks her why she is crying, and she confesses that it is because he is leaving. He is cheered by this, and says that he had come to see if she could care for him, and she says she will. They enjoy the long walk home, in their rainy and muddy state, hands and hearts full, and begin opening their hearts to each other. Friedrich, as Jo now calls him, asks if Jo ever loved Laurie, and Jo explains that she did not. Jo asks why Friedrich decided to visit, and he produces a poem that ran in a newspaper that he recognized as Jo's, and which gave him a glimmer of hope. He intends to go to the West and work, so he can return and provide a home for her, and Jo says she does not mind the wait, or his age, or their poverty, as long as he will help her contribute. Disregarding all social propriety, Jo kisses him on the spot.

Chapter 47 Harvest Time

Jo and her Professor work and wait for a year, writing letters and cultivating their love. When Aunt March dies, she lives her large estate Plumfield to Jo, who has the idea of turning it into a school for boys. She long had the dream of having a school, particularly for orphan boys whom she would love to mother, and shared it with Friedrich, and they agreed to do it once they got rich. Now, with Plumfield, they have the space, Friedrich to teach and Jo to mother, with Father and Mother's advice. Everyone finds it a lovely idea, though Laurie advises that Jo will need rich pupils too, to fund the place. Jo agrees, noting that she already has success raising one such boy to be a successful and admirable man who is accomplished and philanthropic, and says she will make Laurie the model for all her students. Jo is thus married and settled at Plumfield, with a crop of boys rather quickly. Mr. Laurence finds a way to help despite Jo's pride by sending her the poor or orphan boys she wishes and paying their way. Jo has her fill of the boylike life she has always cherished, befriending them and inventing stories for their benefit alone. She and Mr. Bhaer have two sons of their own, Rob and Teddy.

Five years later, the entire family gathers at Plumfield for picking apples and celebrating Mrs. March's sixtieth birthday. The evening ends with a great surprise, with all the pupils singing like angels in the trees a song Jo wrote and Laurie set to music. Afterwards, the sisters all sit together and remember their castles in the air, as well as how differently their lives have turned out. Meg's life is closest to her castle, though her simple home is not full of luxurious things. Jo's life is quite different her dream of being a genius author, though she thinks she may still write a great book yet, informed with all her life's experiences. Amy's castle is also different, but she is blessed by her life and her sweet daughter Beth, although Beth is fragile and weak. The thought of losing her has brought her and Laurie even closer. All agree that they are deeply happy, and Mrs. March is thankful for her happiness and theirs.

Analysis

Despite her promise to Beth, it is difficult for Jo to do her duty to her parents. Jo feels that her sacrifice goes unrewarded, while Amy enjoys her trip abroad. Jo takes comfort in work and in her parents, and Hannah foreshadows that Jo, too, will be rewarded. Indeed Jo is, as marked by the final stage of her growth in womanhood and through Mr. Bhaer's love for her.

This section celebrates the generosity of the Laurences, recalling Marmee saying that money could be used nobly, and Jo telling Laurie in college that if he only spent money helping friends, no one would think the less of him. Now he and his father are exceptionally generous and derive great joy from sharing their wealth. Laurie and Amy's dedication to help "poor gentlefolk" reflect on the situation of the March family - and the Alcott family, who often benefited from the generosity of others.

Part II, in addition to Part I, closes as the beginning of Part I opens, with the March sisters discussing their wishes. Now they are reflecting back on their lives, rather than looking forward. The family is still their core orientation, but the family has grown even more to include children. Even Aunt March has found a place of welcome in the family, through remembrance of her generosity, albeit used differently than she imagined. The granddaughters Daisy and Beth are both reminiscent of the sister Beth, as is Jo's more tempered spirit.

At the close of the book, all feel happy regardless of wealth. Jo is determined to contribute to her household and works in partnership with her husband. She has grown into a "little woman," but enjoys her boys immensely as a mother. The harvest metaphor the girls use to discuss their families in the final paragraphs of the book signifies the hard work and patient cultivation that has one into creating the family's blessings.

Suggested Essay Questions

1. **After Part I of Little Women was published, Alcott received many letters from her readers; one girl wrote that neither she nor her classmates would forgive Alcott if Jo did not marry Laurie. Alcott's journal says that, "girls write to ask who the little women marry, as if that was the only end and aim of a woman's life. I won't marry Jo to Laurie to please anyone." How does Alcott's refusal to have Jo marry Laurie reflect on her own life?**

   Jo was modeled after Alcott, who never married. When Alcott urges her readers to be kind to spinsters, she is speaking from her own experience. Alcott's refusal to meet her readers' demands reflects her own stubbornness, like Jo's. Alcott's decision to have Jo marry at all could reflect a compromise with her readers or perhaps a wish that Alcott's life had gone differently.
2. **Little Women describes the experience of Christian girls growing up in 19th century New England. Yet it continues to be read by people of all ages around the world. What aspects of the book account for its universality?**

   Little Women applies universal, domestic themes of family, love, and self-improvement and to the specific context of the March family. While the girls understand their experiences through the lens of Christianity, people of all cultures and religions can relate to their individual struggles. In addition, the beliefs in the book do not degrade other cultures, but rather promote tolerance and kindness toward all people, as shown by the March family's treatment of Mr. Bhaer, the Hummels, and the war against slavery.
3. **Aunt March and Mr. Laurence are both quite wealthy, but use their wealth differently. Compare the generosity of these figures towards the March family with how this generosity influences their portrayal by Alcott and their perception by other characters.**

   Alcott describes Aunt March as less generous than Mr. Laurence, specifically in the comparison of giving Beth a piano. Yet Aunt March does provide many things to the March family, including giving Meg linens through Aunt Carrol, pays for Amy to travel abroad, and leaves Plumfield to Jo. However, her attitude towards the Marches is one of disdain, and she insults their pride – for example, when she offers to adopt one of the girls. Her generosity is therefore less appreciated because it does not come with her respect. Mr. Laurence is completely respectful of the March family and finds ways to support them without insulting their pride, such as sending Mr. Brooke as an escort on the pretense of business in Washington, and sending boys to Jo's school.
4. **Many critics celebrate Little Women's promotion of women's rights,**

yet the characters adopt very clear gender roles, particularly as husbands and wives. Do the March women demonstrate equality with their husbands?

The words used to describe the roles of husband and wife often suggest mutual helpfulness, but an assumed role for the husband as head of the house, while the actions of the characters highlight women's strength and contributions to the family. Marmee is dependent on Father, yet she runs the house in his absence for almost a year. She also advises Meg to take interest in current events, since they affect her family. Amy calls Laurie "My Lord," but Laurie admits that she guides most of their actions and decisions. Meg is the most submissive of the wives, but Alcott describes her ruling her domestic kingdom. Jo insists on sharing work with her husband, in words and action. Compared to other marriages, such as Sallie and Ned Moffat's, the March women have greater levels of equality with their husbands, though the men are described and perceived as the heads of the household.

5. **Alcott explicitly draws on John Bunyan's Pilgrim's Progress in Part I. Identify and explicate two allusions to Pilgrim's Progress to provide deeper meaning to Alcott's story that may be lost on readers unfamiliar with Bunyan's text.**

   The lions Christian must pass to get to the Palace Beautiful terrify by their roar, but they are in fact chained, and placed their only as tests of faith. So too Beth is frightened of Mr. Laurence's roar, but finds that her fears are unjustified, and that by overcoming her fear she finds not only a piano but also a dear friendship. Apollyon is in fact an external enemy, a demon who attacks Christian. Jo feels that her temper, her "bosom enemy" is almost external in the way it takes control of her, and she must fight it.

6. **When Part I of Little Women was published, the review in The Ladies Repository praised the book for being readable and lively, but warned that "it is not a Christian book. It is religion without spirituality, and salvation without Christ. It is not a good book for the Sunday school library." Is Part I of Little Women a Christian novel?**

   While it may not have adhered to the orthodoxy of the time, Little Women is certainly Christian. Alcott makes heavy allusions to Pilgrim's Progress, the girls seek comfort in their books (argued to be either Pilgrim's Progress or The New Testament), and the entire family seeks comfort from their faith. The light footprint of Christianity in the book, however, helps account for its broad readership.

7. **Drawing on her own travels, Alcott weaves descriptions of the national traits of Germans, British, French, and Italians in her New England-based story. How are her main characters distinctively American?**

At Camp Laurence, the contrast with the British provides an opportunity to display the American traits of the main characters. They play croquet with the spirit of '76, tease Fred for thinking perfectly of the English nation, and John Brooke defends their willingness to work and be independent. Later Laurie brings Meg gifts as examples of "Yankee ingenuity." While abroad, Amy is celebrated for having maintained her "native frankness" despite her other foreign airs. Alcott also describes Demi as respecting the hand that fought him, as did England.

8. **Alcott includes several pieces of writing, such as poems, letters, a newspaper, and a near description of the Christmas play. Discuss the contributions of including these items in the text, rather than simply referring to or describing them.**

   Alcott's story is based on her life and experiences. She believed that if the book would be successful, its success would be due to the honesty of her story – true tales, told in simple language accessible to adolescents. Her inclusion of poems and letters enhances the realism of the book and her characters. After introducing the newspaper, Alcott takes pains to "assure my readers that this is a bona fide copy of one written by bona fide girls."

9. **Alcott's family members were fervent abolitionists, yet the topic of slavery is only vaguely referenced in Little Women. Instead, the oblique references to slavery assume disapproval on the part of the characters and reader. Identify at least two references and discuss the impact of having implicit rather than explicit references.**

   The assumed disapproval of slavery is evident in Mr. March and Mr. Brooke's determination to fight for the Union Army, Jo's quoting of Uncle Tom's Cabin, and Amy's support of the Chester's fair for the freedmen. The vagueness of the references seems intentional; Alcott does not include stories from her childhood such as finding a runaway slave hidden in an unused stove, or her father's school closing when he admitted an African American girl. Keeping references oblique likely increased her readership and avoided distracting from the main parts of the story.

10. **Several of the chapters focus on just one of the sisters. Choose three chapters that focus on the same sister and identify the similarities and differences in the girl's character over time.**

    In Chapters 9, 23, and 28, Alcott describes Meg's attitude towards poverty and her struggles with vanity. Meg never ceases to be aware of her poverty and its affect on her dress and lifestyle – when Amy returns from Paris, Meg envies her dress. However, she learns from experience that she prefers being her genuine self, even in poverty, than aspiring to greater wealth. She first learns this at the Moffat's party, where she is dressed up by her friends like a doll. She then decides to marry John despite his poverty, and sacrifices the support of Aunt March to do so. Enacting this decision, though, is sometimes difficult, as she learns when she overspends on silk for a dress. In the last instance, Meg learns to appreciate poverty and how it has shaped John's character, and thus it shapes her own.

Louisa May Alcott and Her Father

Little Women is largely autobiographical. Deeper understanding of the real experiences in the Alcott family can provide a more nuanced understanding of the characters' relations with one another. The influences of Amos Bronson Alcott, Louisa's father, on the book are extensive. For example, *Pilgrim's Progress*, Louisa's metaphor for the first half of the book, was Bronson's favorite book. Some of Bronson's teaching methods, such as having a student who misbehaved strike him rather than striking the child, are utilized by Mr. Bhaer's character in *Little Men*.

However, Louisa May Alcott's relationship with her father was much more tumultuous than Jo's with the saintly Mr. March was. With greater understanding of Bronson's role in Louisa's life, it is possible to identify remnants of the tension between Louisa and Bronson in the relationship between Jo and her Father.

Bronson Alcott was a fervent philosopher and educator. He believed in Transcendentalism, a diverse movement rooted in New England in the nineteenth century and now associated with Ralph Waldo Emerson and Henry David Thoreau. He both wrote about and tried to live his beliefs. Alcott's philosophy focused on drawing out people's intuitive truth and morality. This belief translated into an educational method that disregarded rote memorization and textbooks in favor of practical learning experiences and the Socratic Method. Bronson applied this method in several experimental schools, most famously the Temple School, which he opened in Boston in 1834. The school flourished until Bronson published *Conversations with the Gospels* in 1836, which described the success of his teaching methods. Unfortunately, *Conversations* was poorly received, as people objected to children engaging in adult conversations. Some parents withdrew their children from Temple School, particularly after Bronson admitted an African American student. The school closed in 1839 and left Bronson deeply in debt.

After living in Concord near Emerson and Thoreau and other philosophers who encouraged Bronson's beliefs, he founded an experimental, communal farm called Fruitlands in 1843. Bronson's strict philosophy, a poor harvest, and ill health all led to the demise of Fruitlands. Bronson was asked to join a Shaker community, which he considered, despite the requirement to separate from his wife and children, as Christian does in *Pilgrim's Progress*. Louisa, who was eleven at the time, remembered this time sadly and prayed that they would stay together. Bronson chose to stay with the family, and after six months at Fruitlands, they moved away. Bronson's depression at the collapse of his utopia was severe. He refused to work as a laborer, could not find a job as a teacher, and fell in the estimation of his friends. Emerson, though he distanced himself publicly from Bronson, supported the family financially for years in the future and eventually helped fund a permanent home for them. Eventually, Bronson was selected as Superintendent of Concord Schools and then started a successful School of Philosophy.

Louisa and her father had a loving respect for one another, yet they caused each other great consternation. Bronson was a perfectionist who made few exceptions for worldly realities. Louisa was wild, impulsive, and strong-tempered, and she frustrated his philosophies. Louisa, for her part, was sometimes angered by her Father's idealism. Louisa described the Fruitlands experiment in a satirical story "Transcendental Wild Oats." This knowledge gives greater meaning to Mr. March's encouragement to Jo to try to write better stories, disregarding the money, and Jo's perseverance in writing her sensation stories in order to pay off the family bills that her own father could not.

At first glance, Mr. March appears as an unworldly and idealistic but good man whose devotion to his family was unwavering. His characterization seems to reflect very little of Louisa's frustration with her father. In Part I, this is partially due to her father's absence. Scholars argue that she reduced and softened his role because he was so unique that readers would have trouble identifying with the family. Yet Bronson was in fact away much of the time, leaving his wife responsible for the household. During one such memorable time at Fruitlands, Bronson and a colleague were away seeking recruits for the farm when a storm threatened the entire barley crop. Taking charge, Louisa's mother directed her children to gather as much barley as they could onto her blankets and sheets before the storm came.

In *Little Women*, none of Jo's frustration at their poverty and the necessity of her work is directed at her father. In truth, Louisa's diary expresses annoyance at his over-extensions of generosity, such as inviting others to stay in their home despite their poverty. She dislikes having to work and sew in order to get by, and is hurt by Bronson's favoritism toward her sisters Anna and May, who are more docile than she is.

With this understanding of Bronson and Louisa's relationship, it is Louisa's portrayal of Mr. March's and Jo's relationship after Beth's death that rings the most true. The time had come when they could talk together as not only father and daughter, but as man and woman, and able and glad to serve each other with mutual sympathy as well as mutual love. With *Little Women*, Louisa was able to pay off her family's debts and gain the respect of the world. When Bronson lectured, he was now introduced as the father of Louisa May Alcott. This new arrangement fostered mutual respect and care in adulthood.

Amos Bronson Alcott died on March 4, 1888. He asked Louisa to "come up with me." Two days later, she did.

Author of ClassicNote and Sources

Elizabeth K. Panarelli, author of ClassicNote. Completed on November 28, 2010, copyright held by GradeSaver.

Updated and revised Bella Wang November 30, 2010. Copyright held by GradeSaver.

Louisa May Alcott. Little Women. New York: New American Library, 2004.

Anne K. Phillips and Gregory Eiselein, editors. Little Women: A Norton Critical Edition. New York: W. W. Norton & Company, Inc., 2004.

John Matteson. Eden's Outcasts: The Story of Louisa May Alcott and Her Father. New York: W. W. Norton & Company, Inc., 2007.

William Anderson. The World of Louisa May Alcott. New York: HarperCollins Publishers, Inc., 1992.

Martha Saxton. Louisa May Alcott: A Modern Biography. New York: Farrar, Straus and Giroux, 1995.

Joel Myerson, Daniel Shealy and Madeleine B. Stern, editors. The Selected Letters of Louisa May Alcott. Athens, Georgia: University of Georgia Press, 1995.

Linda K. Kerber, Alice Kesslr-Harris, and Kathryn Kish Sklar, editors. U.S. History as Women's History: New Feminist Essays. Chapel Hill: University of North Carolina Press, 1995.

Quiz 1

1. **Which of the sisters likes to draw and is called "little Raphael?"**
   A. Jo
   B. Meg
   C. Amy
   D. Beth

2. **When Meg and Jo go to Mrs. Gardiner's New Year's Ball, they have to share which item, because Jo spoiled hers?**
   A. Meg's umbrella
   B. Meg's winter coat
   C. Meg's handkerchief
   D. Meg's gloves

3. **When Jo tries to curl Meg's hair for the New Year's party, instead she does what?**
   A. Dyes it
   B. Frizzes it
   C. Flattens it
   D. Burns it off

4. **Who eats the March family's Christmas breakfast?**
   A. Soldiers at the hospital on Boston
   B. Hannah's family
   C. Slaves on the underground railroad
   D. The Hummels, a nearby German family

5. **What is the March family tradition before going to bed?**
   A. Reading from The Bible
   B. Saying the Lord's Prayer
   C. Taking cold baths
   D. Singing together

6. **Amy gets in trouble at school for having which items in her desk?**
   A. Pickled limes
   B. Kittens
   C. Answer sheets to quizzes
   D. Drawings of Mr. Davis

7. **What is Laurie's first name?**
   A. Robert
   B. Laurence
   C. Theodore
   D. John

8. **Whom does Beth remind Mr. Laurence of?**
   A. His mother
   B. His sister
   C. His daughter-in-law, an Italian musician
   D. His granddaughter

9. **Why is the March family poor?**
   A. They spend all their money on books
   B. They have no sons to help earn money
   C. Mr. March lost his property helping a friend
   D. Mr. March gambled too much and lost

10. **What does Aunt March call Jo, to Jo's dismay?**
   A. Miss March
   B. Josy-phine
   C. Girl
   D. Joanna

11. **How does Jo win a prize of $100?**
   A. Saving a wealthy boy from drowning
   B. Growing the largest squash in town
   C. Acting in a play
   D. Writing a story about an earthquake in Lisbon

12. **Why does Aunt Carrol invite Amy to Europe, instead of Jo?**
   A. Jo offended Aunt Carrol while calling on Aunt March
   B. Aunt Carrol doesn't like Jo's writings
   C. Amy begged Aunt Carrol to take her
   D. Jo is ill at the time

13. **For Christmas, all the sisters decide to give presents to whom?**
   A. The Soldiers' Aid Society
   B. The Hummels
   C. Themselves
   D. Marmee

14. **How does Amy remind herself not to be selfish after Beth gets sick?**
   A. Singing Beth's favorite hymn
   B. Praying with a rosary
   C. Cutting her hair
   D. Wearing a turquoise ring

15. **Why doesn't Jo marry Laurie?**
   A. Laurie never asks her
   B. She thinks he loves Beth
   C. She is uncomfortable with his wealth
   D. They are both too strong-willed

16. **Why did Laurie's father run away?**
   A. To join the war
   B. He lost his money gambling and was ashamed
   C. He hated the family business
   D. He married an Italian musician

17. **What game do the girls play during the year their Father is gone?**
   A. Cricket
   B. Authors
   C. Rig-marole
   D. Pilgrim's Progress

18. **What great character flaw does Marmee reveal to Jo she has also struggled with?**
   A. Vanity
   B. A fiery temper
   C. Shyness
   D. Laziness

19. **How does Beth thank Mr. Laurence for letting her play his piano?**
    A. She writes him a letter
    B. She makes him a pair of slippers
    C. She makes him blancmange
    D. She composes a song for him

20. **How does Amy punish Jo for not letting her come to the theater?**
    A. She empties out Jo's clothes dresser
    B. She hides a rat in Jo's bed
    C. She burns Jo's book manuscript
    D. She throws away Jo's skates

21. **What happens when Laurie sees Meg dressed up in style at the Moffats' party?**
    A. He runs to get her a glass of champagne
    B. He falls in love with her
    C. He becomes shy and hides from her
    D. He tells her he doesn't like how she looks

22. **As thanks for his acceptance into the Pickwick Club, what gift does Laurie present?**
    A. A piano
    B. New copies of all of Dickens's books
    C. A post office between their houses
    D. Each of their favorite flowers

23. **Who inspires Meg to declare her love for John Brooke?**
    A. Laurie
    B. Ned Moffat
    C. Her Father
    D. Aunt March

24. **Before John and Meg can marry, what duty must John fulfill?**
    A. Caring for his ailing mother
    B. Tutoring Laurie until he finishes college
    C. Fighting in the Union Army
    D. Paying off his debt to Mr. Laurence

25. **Who is the narrator of the book?**

A. Mr. March

B. Jo

C. Mrs. March

D. Louisa May Alcott

Quiz 1 Answer Key

1. **(C)** Amy
2. **(D)** Meg's gloves
3. **(D)** Burns it off
4. **(D)** The Hummels, a nearby German family
5. **(D)** Singing together
6. **(A)** Pickled limes
7. **(C)** Theodore
8. **(D)** His granddaughter
9. **(C)** Mr. March lost his property helping a friend
10. **(B)** Josy-phine
11. **(D)** Writing a story about an earthquake in Lisbon
12. **(A)** Jo offended Aunt Carrol while calling on Aunt March
13. **(D)** Marmee
14. **(D)** Wearing a turquoise ring
15. **(D)** They are both too strong-willed
16. **(D)** He married an Italian musician
17. **(D)** Pilgrim's Progress
18. **(B)** A fiery temper
19. **(B)** She makes him a pair of slippers
20. **(C)** She burns Jo's book manuscript
21. **(D)** He tells her he doesn't like how she looks
22. **(C)** A post office between their houses
23. **(D)** Aunt March
24. **(C)** Fighting in the Union Army
25. **(D)** Louisa May Alcott

Quiz 2

1. **Despite requests from her readers, what did Alcott refuse to make Jo do?**
   A. Save Beth's life
   B. Marry Laurie
   C. Go to college
   D. Run away disguised as a boy

2. **What item does Meg think she loses, but is in fact in John Brooke's pocket?**
   A. A glove
   B. A handkerchief
   C. A portrait of her by Amy
   D. A copy of a German song she translated

3. **Which character is modeled after Louisa May Alcott?**
   A. Jo
   B. Mrs. March
   C. Meg
   D. Aunt March

4. **At Camp Laurence, during which game does Jo catch Fred Vaughn cheating?**
   A. Cricket
   B. Croquet
   C. Authors
   D. Hide and seek

5. **Why does Amy give up on being a famous artist?**
   A. She decides ambition is not ladylike
   B. She gets married
   C. She is rejected from the best art school
   D. She recognizes her talent is not genius

6. **What is Amy's impression of Laurie when they spend Christmas in Nice?**
   A. She admires his recovery from Jo's rejection
   B. She enjoys his flattery and tries to flirt with him
   C. She finds him unchanged from their childhood
   D. She despises his laziness

7. **On her wedding day, what promise does Meg extract from Laurie?**
   A. Not to play billiards
   B. Not to run away from his grandfather
   C. Not to drink
   D. Not to gamble

8. **What precedes Meg and John's first big fight?**
   A. Meg's attempt to make currant jelly
   B. Meg ruining a lobster dinner
   C. Meg running home to gossip with her family
   D. Meg tiring of hearing about politics

9. **Jo goes to New York because she thinks Beth loves Laurie. What is Beth's real secret?**
   A. She wants to go to school for music
   B. She envies Amy for going abroad
   C. She thinks Mr. Laurence is dying
   D. She believes she is dying

10. **Why is Jo upset when Meg and John get engaged?**
   A. She hates to lose Meg and have the family split up
   B. She wants Meg to marry Ned Moffat
   C. She does not respect John
   D. She thinks John is too poor

11. **In order to send her father money when he is sick, what does Jo do?**
   A. Begs Aunt March for the money
   B. Cuts and sells her hair
   C. Writes and sells a book
   D. Borrows money from Laurie

12. **When Beth gets sick with scarlet fever, why doesn't Hannah tell Mrs. March?**
   A. Beth is not very sick
   B. She fears Mrs. March will blame her for Beth's illness
   C. It is not proper for Mrs. March to travel alone
   D. She fears Mr. March will get worse if Mrs. March comes home

13. **How does Laurie convince Amy to stay at Aunt March's when Beth is sick?**
   A. By describing scarlet fever in gruesome detail
   B. By bribing her with drawing lessons
   C. By promising to come visit every day
   D. By striking her palm for being selfish

14. **What is the March family's greatest Christmas surprise?**
   A. John Brooke proposing to Meg
   B. An organ for Beth
   C. A feast from the Hummels
   D. Father coming home from the hospital

15. **How does Jo spend her earnings from writing?**
   A. Buying a horse
   B. Sending Beth to the shore to get well
   C. Expanding her library
   D. Buying Meg her first silk dress

16. **What does Jo plan to do with Plumfield after Aunt March wills it to her?**
   A. Open a school for boys
   B. Sell it an buy a simple home for her and Fritz
   C. Open a boardinghouse like Mrs. Kirke's
   D. Move her entire family there, so they can be together

17. **How does Jo get her revenge on the Chesters for mistreating Amy at the fair?**
   A. Publishing a satire of May Chester in the town newspaper
   B. Turning Meg Chester's table on its side
   C. Sending Laurie and his friends to make Amy's table the most popular
   D. Organizing a boycott of the fair

18. **Why does Amy turn down Fred Vaughn's marriage proposal?**
   A. She does not want to live in England
   B. She has already accepted Laurie's proposal
   C. She remembers him cheating at Camp Laurence
   D. She realizes she wants to marry for more than money

19. **How does Meg react after her purchase of silk for a dress upsets John?**
    A. She sells the material and buys a coat for him
    B. She considers leaving him, as she is tired of poverty
    C. She vows never to wear silk again
    D. She starts working as a governess again

20. **When their babies are one year old, why does John spend most evenings away from Meg?**
    A. He is working late to pay for the new costs
    B. Meg is always in the nursery
    C. He is in love with another woman
    D. He believes raising children is Meg's responsibility

21. **During his last year of college, what motivates Laurie to work hard and graduate with honors?**
    A. Mr. March's admonitions to make the most of his education
    B. A truly inspiring professor
    C. Trying to get a job outside his grandfather's company
    D. Trying to impress Jo and be worthy of her

22. **When Mr. Bhaer comes to visit, for whom does he ask at the door?**
    A. Mr. March
    B. Jo
    C. Mrs. March
    D. Demi and Daisy

23. **On Mr. Bhaer's last day in Concord, where does he tell Jo he is going to teach?**
    A. Back in Germany
    B. With a family in Concord
    C. At Harvard
    D. In a college out West

24. **What trait does Jo credit with making Mr. Bhaer univerally liked?**
    A. Witty sense of humor
    B. Unfailing benevolence
    C. Intellectual brilliance
    D. Impressive foreign ideas

25. **In return for Jo mending his socks, what does Mr. Bhaer give her?**
   A. A writing desk
   B. German lessons
   C. A book of poetry
   D. Theater tickets

Quiz 2 Answer Key

1. **(B)** Marry Laurie
2. **(A)** A glove
3. **(A)** Jo
4. **(B)** Croquet
5. **(D)** She recognizes her talent is not genius
6. **(D)** She despises his laziness
7. **(C)** Not to drink
8. **(A)** Meg's attempt to make currant jelly
9. **(D)** She believes she is dying
10. **(A)** She hates to lose Meg and have the family split up
11. **(B)** Cuts and sells her hair
12. **(D)** She fears Mr. March will get worse if Mrs. March comes home
13. **(C)** By promising to come visit every day
14. **(D)** Father coming home from the hospital
15. **(B)** Sending Beth to the shore to get well
16. **(A)** Open a school for boys
17. **(C)** Sending Laurie and his friends to make Amy's table the most popular
18. **(D)** She realizes she wants to marry for more than money
19. **(A)** She sells the material and buys a coat for him
20. **(B)** Meg is always in the nursery
21. **(D)** Trying to impress Jo and be worthy of her
22. **(A)** Mr. March
23. **(D)** In a college out West
24. **(B)** Unfailing benevolence
25. **(B)** German lessons

Quiz 3

1. **How does Mr. Bhaer react when he guesses Jo is writing sensation stories?**
   A. Suggesting she speak to a publisher he knows
   B. Minding his own business
   C. Saying he wishes honest people wouldn't produce such filth
   D. Congratulting her on her success

2. **What prompts Mr. Bhaer come to Concord to visit Jo?**
   A. A letter Jo writes to him
   B. News of Laurie and Amy's marriage
   C. A poem she wrote that he reads in the newspaper
   D. His nephews going to college, leaving him alone

3. **Why does Jo give up her dream of being a famous author?**
   A. She feels guilty about writing sensation stories
   B. Beth asks Jo to care for Mother and Father when she dies
   C. Publishers won't accept female authors
   D. Criticism of her first book is too harsh

4. **What is Beth's burden she tries to overcome while Father is gone?**
   A. To become less bashful
   B. To stop envying Am y for going to school
   C. To learn to play the piano
   D. To take care of the Hummels

5. **When Father comes home, he compliments Meg for having ___?**
   A. Beautifully embroidered handkerchiefs
   B. Burnt hands, which show her hard work
   C. Improved in German, despite his absence
   D. Pretty new dresses

6. **Why is living without luxuries sometimes harder for Meg than for her sisters?**
   A. Meg remembers when the family was rich
   B. Meg is concerned about having suitors
   C. Meg dislikes simple foods
   D. Meg thinks women should not have to work

7. **What is Beth's one worry before she dies?**
    A. She never got to se the ocean
    B. Her piano will go out of tune
    C. No one will look after her dolls
    D. She has wasted her life and not done enough for anyone

8. **In Vienna, what does Laurie realize?**
    A. He should have studied music here instead of going to college
    B. He will never stop wanting to marry Jo
    C. He should model his music after Mozart
    D. He does not have a genius for music

9. **How does Amy respond when she learns Beth has died?**
    A. She immediately makes arrangements to go home
    B. She goes to visit Laurie in London
    C. She waits for Laurie to come to her
    D. She makes a bust of Beth to remember her by

10. **Where does Laurie propose to Amy?**
    A. In the Louvre in Paris
    B. On a lake, while rowing a boat together
    C. At Valrosa, where she sketched and lectured him
    D. In the garden in Vevey at midnight

11. **Why did Louisa May Alcott write Little Women?**
    A. To pay off her gambling debts
    B. To counteract the anti-feminist literature at the time
    C. An editor asked her to write a book for girls
    D. As a friendly competition with a friend writing a boys' book

12. **What opens Jo's heart to the prospect of marriage?**
    A. Seeing Meg so happy with her babies
    B. Her sad experience nursing and losing Beth
    C. Her loneliness with everyone else married or gone
    D. All of these choices

13. **Where does Mr. Bhaer propose?**
   A. Under an umbrella walking home from town
   B. In a poem he wrote for Jo
   C. In the train station before he leaves
   D. Over tea in the March house

14. **How old is Mr. Bhaer when Jo meets him?**
   A. Almost 30
   B. Almost 40
   C. Almost 50
   D. Almost 60

15. **How does Mr. Laurence find a way to support Jo without hurting her pride?**
   A. Paying for poor students to attend her school
   B. Asking her and Mr. Bhaer to live in one of his properties
   C. Anonymously doubling Mr. Bhaer's salary at the college
   D. Buying Plumfield from her at a good price

16. **Why do Laurie and Amy get married in Europe?**
   A. They are afraid Mr. Laurence may not survive the journey
   B. They are afraid Amy's parents won't approve
   C. So Amy can travel alone with the Laurences back to the States
   D. Amy is afraid Laurie will love Jo again when he sees her

17. **What is the one "shadow" in Amy's married life?**
   A. Laurie is very preoccupied with business
   B. Her daughter Beth is very weak
   C. She has no opportunities or time to make art
   D. She hates living so far from home

18. **When does Mr. March first realize Mr. Bhaer has feelings for Jo?**
   A. When he sees Mr. Bhaer's expression while he sings to the family
   B. When Mr. March sees them kissing under the umbrell
   C. When Demi asks Mr. Bhaer if boys like girls
   D. When Jo confides in him, asking his advice

19. **What surprise does her family plan for Mrs. March's sixtieth birthday?**
    A. The girls give her the same gifts as in the first Christmas in the book
    B. Jo's students sing to her from the treetops of the orchard
    C. Jo and Laurie build her a snowman
    D. Amy and Laurie get married

20. **What scandalizes Aunt March at Meg's wedding?**
    A. Mr. March is the celebrant, which isn't proper
    B. Everyone is drinking heavily
    C. There aren't enough flowers, since they were too expensive
    D. She is welcomed by Meg, who is seen before the ceremoney

21. **What helps Mrs. March learn to control her temper?**
    A. Her mother
    B. Being a good example for her daughters
    C. Her husband
    D. All of these choices

22. **When Jo does anything improper in public, how does Meg signal to her?**
    A. Raising her eyebrows
    B. Winking
    C. Tapping her foot
    D. Speaking their codeword

23. **When Amy is inspired to be good at Christmas, how does she try to be less selfish?**
    A. Playing Christmas carols so Beth can rest
    B. Pricking her fingers sewing for the soldiers
    C. Giving away her drawing pencils
    D. Exchanging a small cologne bottle for Marmee for a larger one

24. **What trait of Jo's does Amy urge her to stop?**
    A. Talking slang
    B. Cooking poorly
    C. Showing off with French words
    D. Writing plays Amy has to act in

25. **After proposing Laurie's entrance to the Pickwick Club, how does Jo surprise the girls?**
   A. By announcing Laurie will take her place, she's quitting
   B. By revealing Laurie in hiding
   C. By revealing her hair cut short
   D. By announcing she submitted a story from the paper to be published

Quiz 3 Answer Key

1. **(C)** Saying he wishes honest people wouldn't produce such filth
2. **(C)** A poem she wrote that he reads in the newspaper
3. **(B)** Beth asks Jo to care for Mother and Father when she dies
4. **(A)** To become less bashful
5. **(B)** Burnt hands, which show her hard work
6. **(A)** Meg remembers when the family was rich
7. **(D)** She has wasted her life and not done enough for anyone
8. **(D)** He does not have a genius for music
9. **(C)** She waits for Laurie to come to her
10. **(B)** On a lake, while rowing a boat together
11. **(C)** An editor asked her to write a book for girls
12. **(D)** All of these choices
13. **(A)** Under an umbrella walking home from town
14. **(A)** Almost 30
15. **(A)** Paying for poor students to attend her school
16. **(C)** So Amy can travel alone with the Laurences back to the States
17. **(B)** Her daughter Beth is very weak
18. **(C)** When Demi asks Mr. Bhaer if boys like girls
19. **(B)** Jo's students sing to her from the treetops of the orchard
20. **(D)** She is welcomed by Meg, who is seen before the ceremoney
21. **(D)** All of these choices
22. **(A)** Raising her eyebrows
23. **(D)** Exchanging a small cologne bottle for Marmee for a larger one
24. **(A)** Talking slang
25. **(B)** By revealing Laurie in hiding

Quiz 4

1. **When the girls perform plays, how do they manage male roles**
   A. Jo rewrites the plays to take out the male roles
   B. Jo plays boy's roles to her hearts delight
   C. They avoid plays with male roles until Laurie joins their group
   D. Mrs. March asks them to perform all female plays to avoid thinking about romance

2. **In what year was Little Women published in full, with both parts?**
   A. 1849
   B. 1869
   C. 1899
   D. 1909

3. **What nickname does Amy use for Laurie?**
   A. My lord
   B. Dora
   C. Mr. Laurence
   D. Teddy

4. **What does Jo love most about working for Aunt March?**
   A. The extensive library
   B. Her parrot
   C. Her walk to work in the fresh air
   D. The challenge of making Aunt March laugh

5. **What funny gift does Beth send on Jo's first visit to the Laurence house?**
   A. A baked potato
   B. A passage from The Bible
   C. Her kittens
   D. A song she composed

6. **What does Laurie send to Jo with the invitation to Camp Laurence?**
   A. A hiking stick
   B. A big floppy hat
   C. A croquet mallet
   D. An oar for the boat

7. **When Jo rejects Laurie, what plan does Mr. Laurence smartly propose?**
   A. Laurie and Mr. Laurence travel to Europe together
   B. Laurie throw himself into business
   C. Laurie try wooing Amy instead
   D. Laurie travel alone for awhile

8. **When Jo and Laurie talk at the New Year's Party, why is Jo avoiding dancing?**
   A. The back of her dress is burnt
   B. Her shoes are too tight and they hurt
   C. She hates to dance
   D. She does not know how to dance properly

9. **While preparing a nice fete for her classmates from art school, what is Amy carrying when she unfortunately runs into one of Laurie's friends?**
   A. A nude portrait
   B. A lobster
   C. Used decorations from a friend's party
   D. None of these choices

10. **Where do Laurie and Amy spend their honeymoon?**
    A. Boston
    B. New York
    C. Valrosa
    D. Rome

11. **When Mr. March returns from the war, where does he find work?**
    A. As a bookkeeper for Mr. Laurence's trading company
    B. As a teacher in a school for freedmen
    C. As a shopkeeper in town
    D. As a minister at a nearby parish

12. **When Laurie sees Jo going to the newspaperman in town, what does he think she is doing?**
    A. Objecting to an immoral story the paper ran
    B. Buying him a birthday present
    C. Having teeth out at the dentist
    D. Playing billiards

13. **What branch of philosophy did Amos Bronson Alcott pursue?**
    A. Stoicism
    B. Speculative Philosophy
    C. Kantianism
    D. Transcendentalism

14. **When Jo feels despairing after Beth dies, what does Marmee encourage her to do?**
    A. Reconsider marrying Laurie
    B. Learn to play the piano
    C. Try writing again
    D. Learn to cook

15. **How does Jo surprise the other residents at Mrs. Kirke's boardinghouse?**
    A. Receiving male visitors alone in her room
    B. Defending religion and morality durin ga philosophical discussion
    C. Acting sociable and outgoing at the masquerade ball
    D. Revealing that she is the author of the sensation stories in the Weekly Volcano

16. **What experiement do the girls try on their first week of vacation?**
    A. Cooking all of their own food
    B. Avoiding all work and enjoying only leisure
    C. Swapping their usual chores with each other
    D. Speaking in German to improve their language skills

17. **What role does Mr. March have in the Union Army?**
    A. He is a colonel
    B. He is a chaplain
    C. He trains freedmen soldiers
    D. He is a spy

18. **What do the girls carry with them as muffs in the cold?**
    A. Kittens
    B. Baked potatoes
    C. Newspapers
    D. Old slippers

19. **Despite her vow not to give Meg a penny if she married John Brooke, what does Aunt March pay for Aunt Carrol to give to Meg?**
   A. A set of pearls
   B. A trip to Europe
   C. A honeymoon
   D. A full set of linens

20. **What does Mr. March buy with the money Jo sends him from cutting her hair?**
   A. Nothing
   B. Medicine
   C. Wine
   D. Shakespeare

21. **When Mr. Brooke first tells Mr. and Mrs. March about his feelings for Meg, how do they respond?**
   A. They congratulate him and arrange the marriage
   B. They refuse, not approving of tutors
   C. They tell Meg right away, so she can make her own choice
   D. Meg is too young to be engaged yet

22. **Which trait does Louisa May Alcott stress as distinctly American throughout the book?**
   A. Independence
   B. Economic savvy
   C. Morality
   D. Piety

23. **When Jo writes her first book, on what condition does the publisher accept it?**
   A. She includes illustrations, which Amy draws
   B. She cuts one third of the length
   C. She removes all references to slavery
   D. She changes the heroine to a hero

24. **On what pretense does Jo first visit the Laurence house?**
   A. Asking to borrow their boat
   B. Cheering up Laurie, who has a bad cold
   C. Examining their library
   D. Returning a runaway pony

25. **Who is Beth's favorite doll?**

A. Abby
B. Minna
C. Lotty
D. Joanna

Quiz 4 Answer Key

1. **(B)** Jo plays boy's roles to her hearts delight
2. **(B)** 1869
3. **(A)** My lord
4. **(A)** The extensive library
5. **(C)** Her kittens
6. **(B)** A big floppy hat
7. **(A)** Laurie and Mr. Laurence travel to Europe together
8. **(A)** The back of her dress is burnt
9. **(B)** A lobster
10. **(C)** Valrosa
11. **(D)** As a minister at a nearby parish
12. **(C)** Having teeth out at the dentist
13. **(D)** Transcendentalism
14. **(C)** Try writing again
15. **(C)** Acting sociable and outgoing at the masquerade ball
16. **(B)** Avoiding all work and enjoying only leisure
17. **(B)** He is a chaplain
18. **(B)** Baked potatoes
19. **(D)** A full set of linens
20. **(A)** Nothing
21. **(D)** Meg is too young to be engaged yet
22. **(A)** Independence
23. **(B)** She cuts one third of the length
24. **(B)** Cheering up Laurie, who has a bad cold
25. **(D)** Joanna

ClassicNotes

GradeSaver™

Getting you the grade since 1999™

Other ClassicNotes from GradeSaver™

Silas Marner
Sir Gawain and the Green Knight
Sister Carrie
Six Characters in Search of an Author
Slaughterhouse Five
Snow Falling on Cedars
The Social Contract
Something Wicked This Way Comes
Song of Roland
Song of Solomon
Songs of Innocence and of Experience
Sons and Lovers
The Sorrows of Young Werther
The Sound and the Fury
The Spanish Tragedy
Spenser's Amoretti and Epithalamion
Spring Awakening
The Stranger
A Streetcar Named Desire
Sula
The Sun Also Rises
Tale of Two Cities
The Taming of the Shrew
The Tempest
Tender is the Night
Tess of the D'Urbervilles
Their Eyes Were Watching God
Things Fall Apart
The Things They Carried
A Thousand Splendid Suns
The Threepenny Opera
Through the Looking Glass
Thus Spoke Zarathustra
The Time Machine
Titus Andronicus
To Build a Fire
To Kill a Mockingbird
To the Lighthouse
The Tortilla Curtain
Touching Spirit Bear
Treasure Island
Trifles
Troilus and Cressida
Tropic of Cancer
Tropic of Capricorn
Tuesdays With Morrie
The Turn of the Screw
Twelfth Night
Twilight
Ulysses
Uncle Tom's Cabin
Utopia
Vanity Fair
A Very Old Man With Enormous Wings
Villette
The Visit
Volpone
Waiting for Godot
Waiting for Lefty
Walden
Washington Square
The Waste Land
The Wealth of Nations
Where the Red Fern Grows
White Fang
A White Heron and Other Stories
White Noise
White Teeth
Who's Afraid of Virginia Woolf
Wide Sargasso Sea
Wieland
Winesburg, Ohio
The Winter's Tale
The Woman Warrior
Wordsworth's Poetical Works
Woyzeck
A Wrinkle in Time
Wuthering Heights
The Yellow Wallpaper
Yonnondio: From the Thirties
Zeitoun

For our full list of over 250 Study Guides, Quizzes, Sample College Application Essays, Literature Essays and E-texts, visit:

www.gradesaver.com

Made in the USA
Coppell, TX
22 January 2020

14891409R00066